TIME OUT

Pool League Shots

52 Drills with Over 150 Shots

For Every Skill Level Player

By Drill Instructor

DOMINIC ESPOSITO

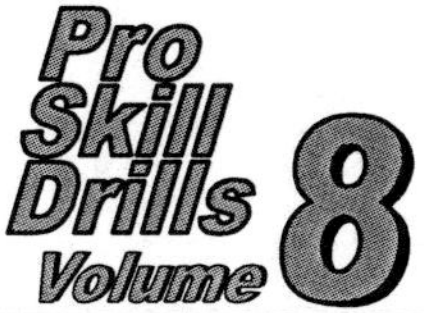

Need TIME OUT Help?
Call Me at:
407-927-1484

POOL Tables
of Contents

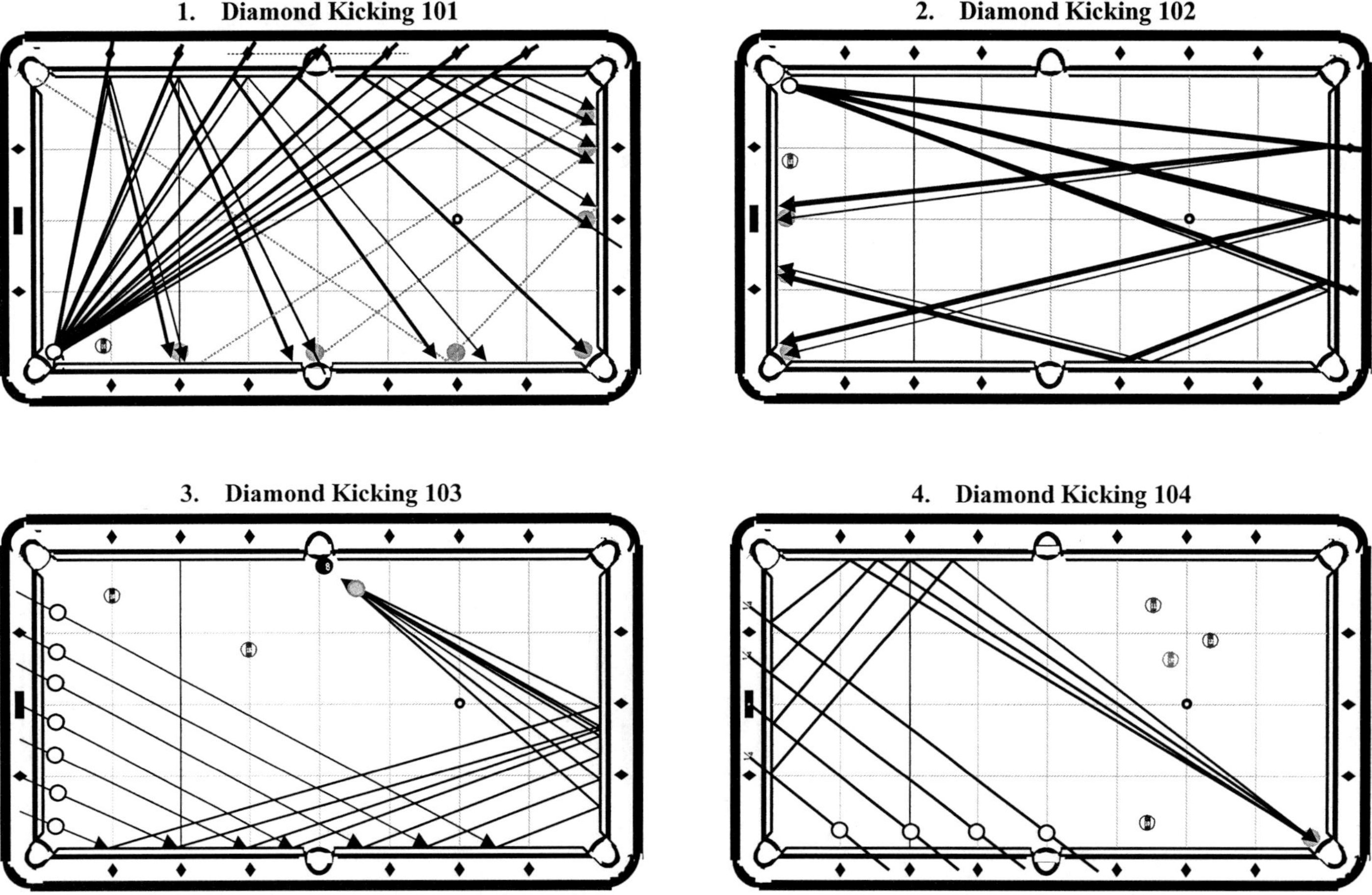
1. Diamond Kicking 101
2. Diamond Kicking 102
3. Diamond Kicking 103
4. Diamond Kicking 104

5. Short Rail Kick - Inside English

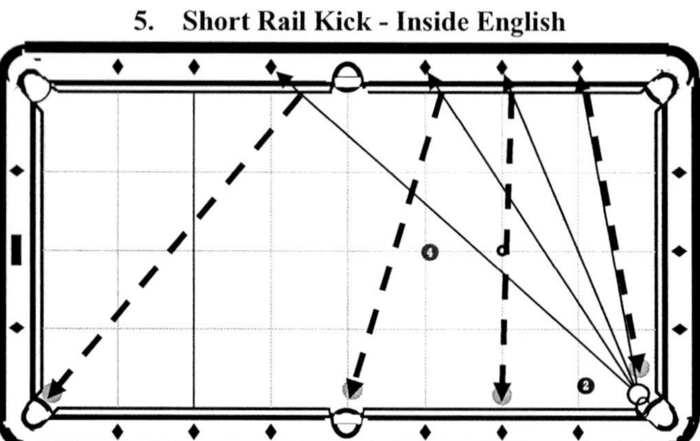

6. One Rail Kick—Inside English

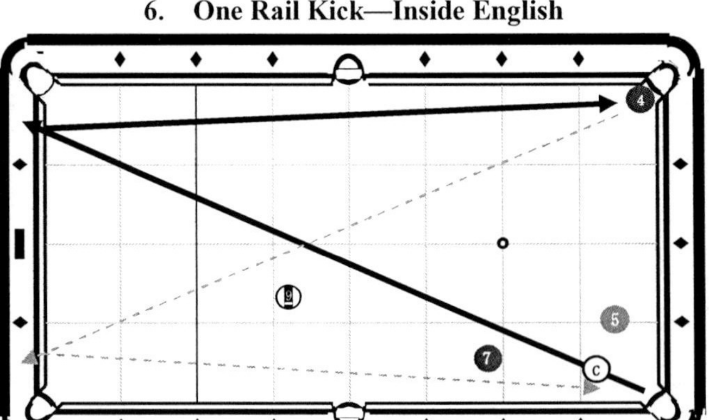

7. Two Rail Kick—Inside English

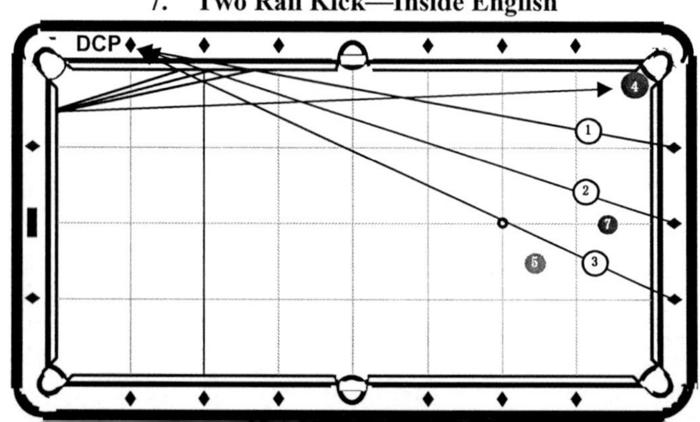

8. Kicking By TIPS of English 1

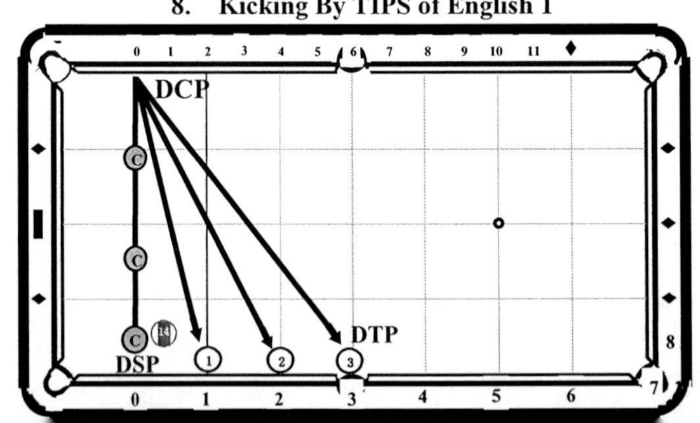

9. Kicking By TIPS of English 2

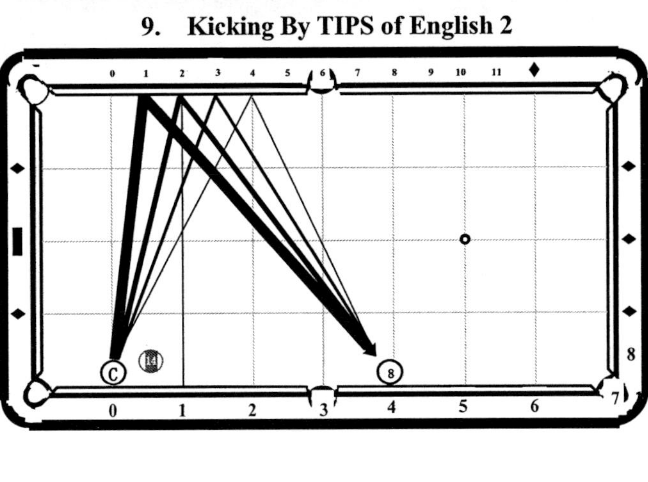

10. Kicking By TIPS of English 3

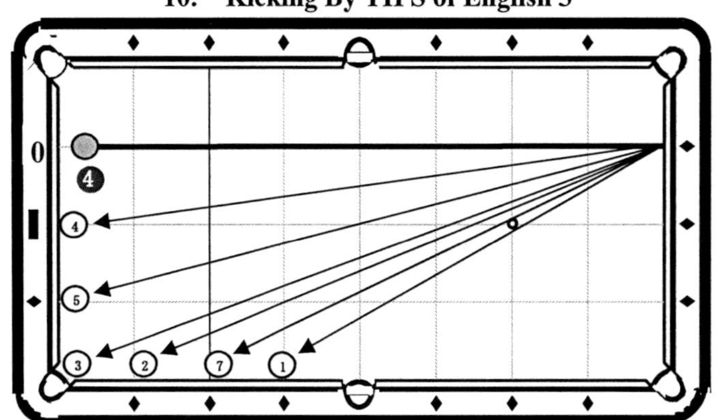

11. 1 Rail Kick - Cue Ball LOW

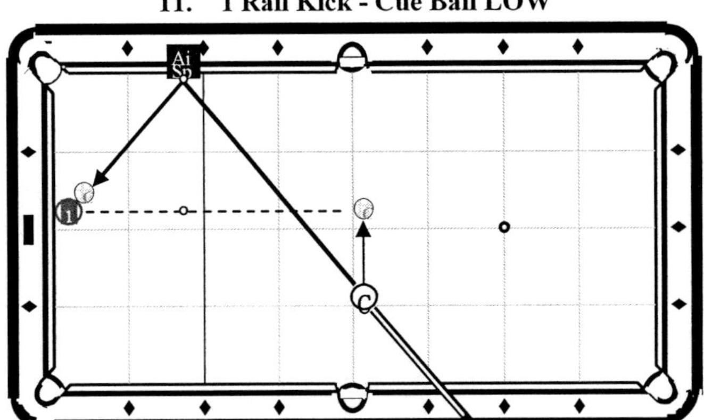

12. 1 Rail Kick - Cue Ball HIGH

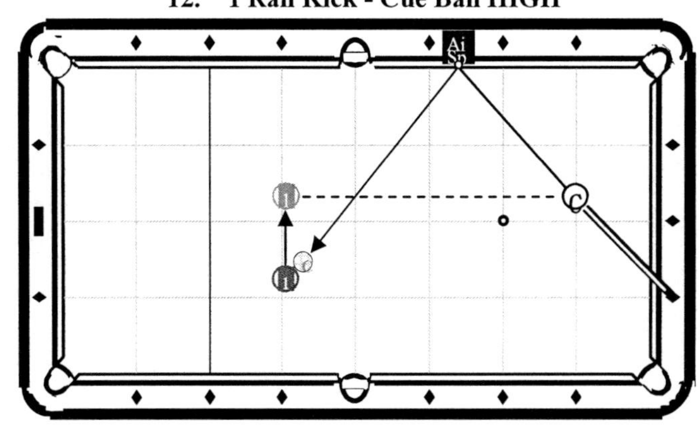

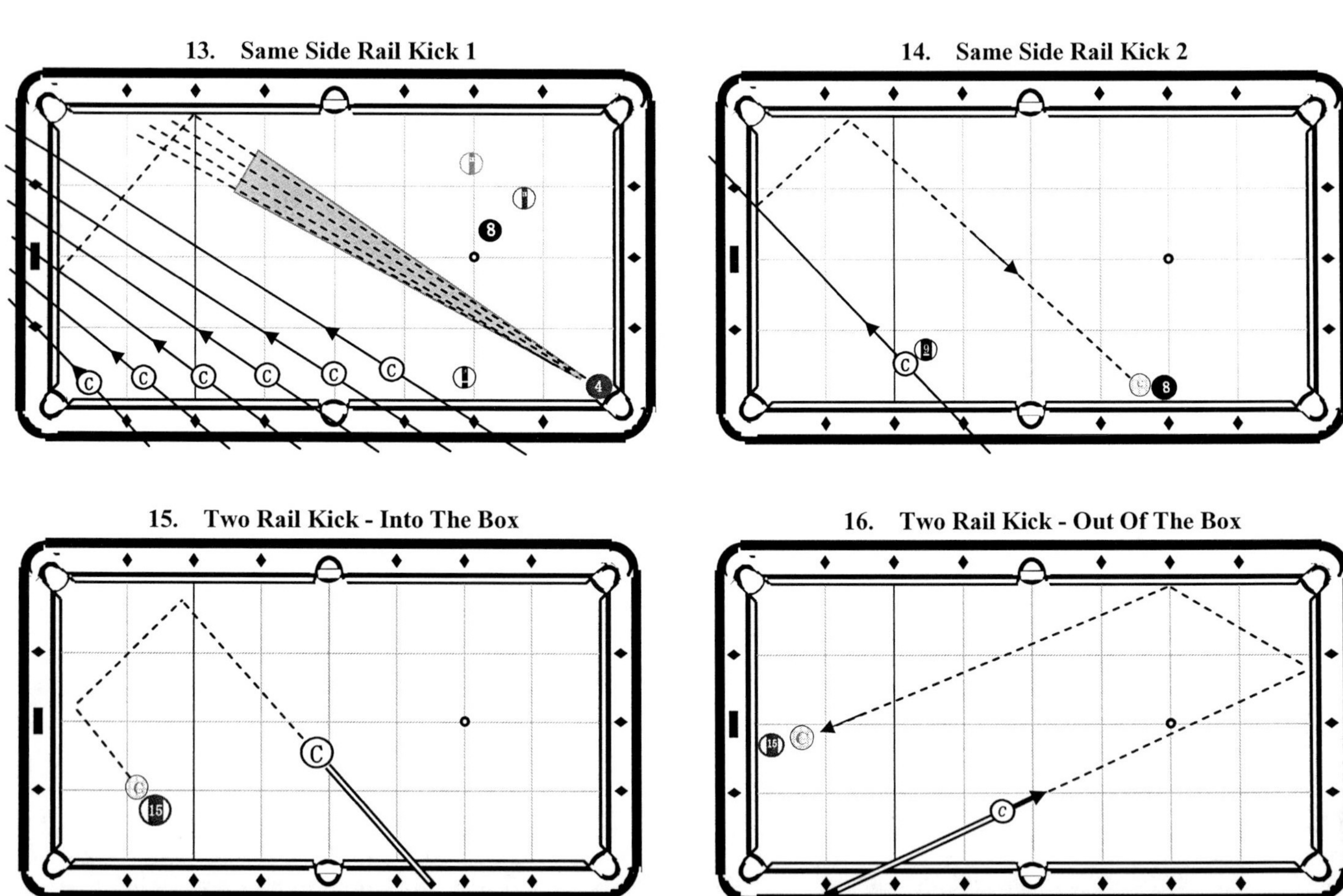
13. Same Side Rail Kick 1
8
C
4
14. Same Side Rail Kick 2
9
C
8
15. Two Rail Kick - Into The Box
C
15
16. Two Rail Kick - Out Of The Box
15
C

17. Rail First Kick Shot 1

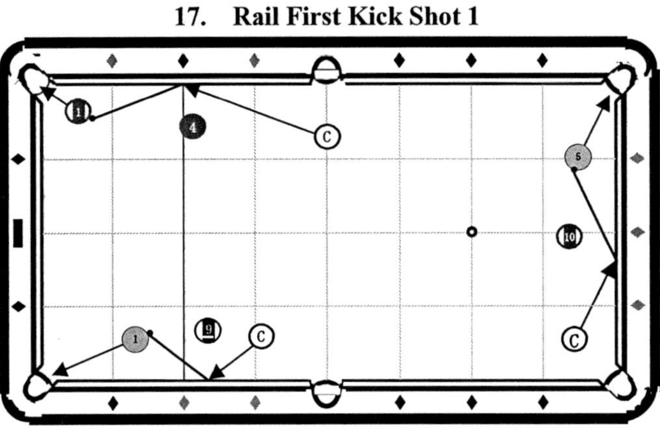

18. Rail First Kick Shot 2

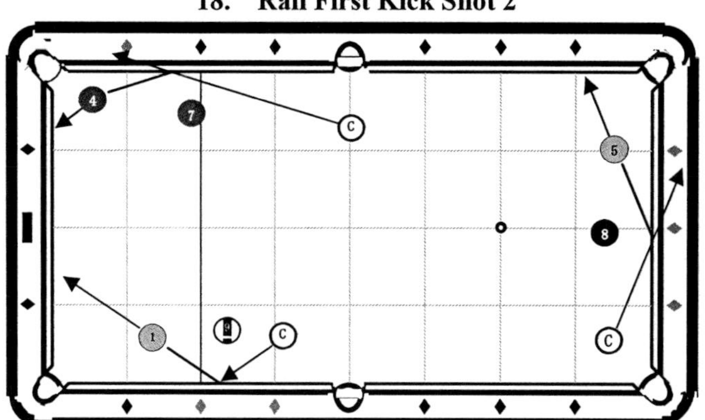

19. Frozen Shots 1

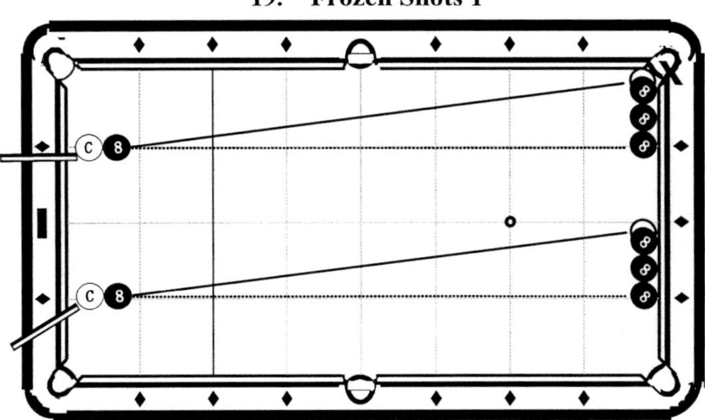

20. Frozen Shots 2

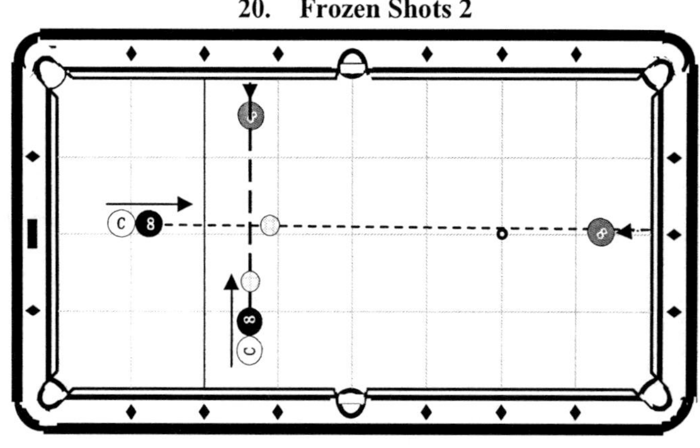

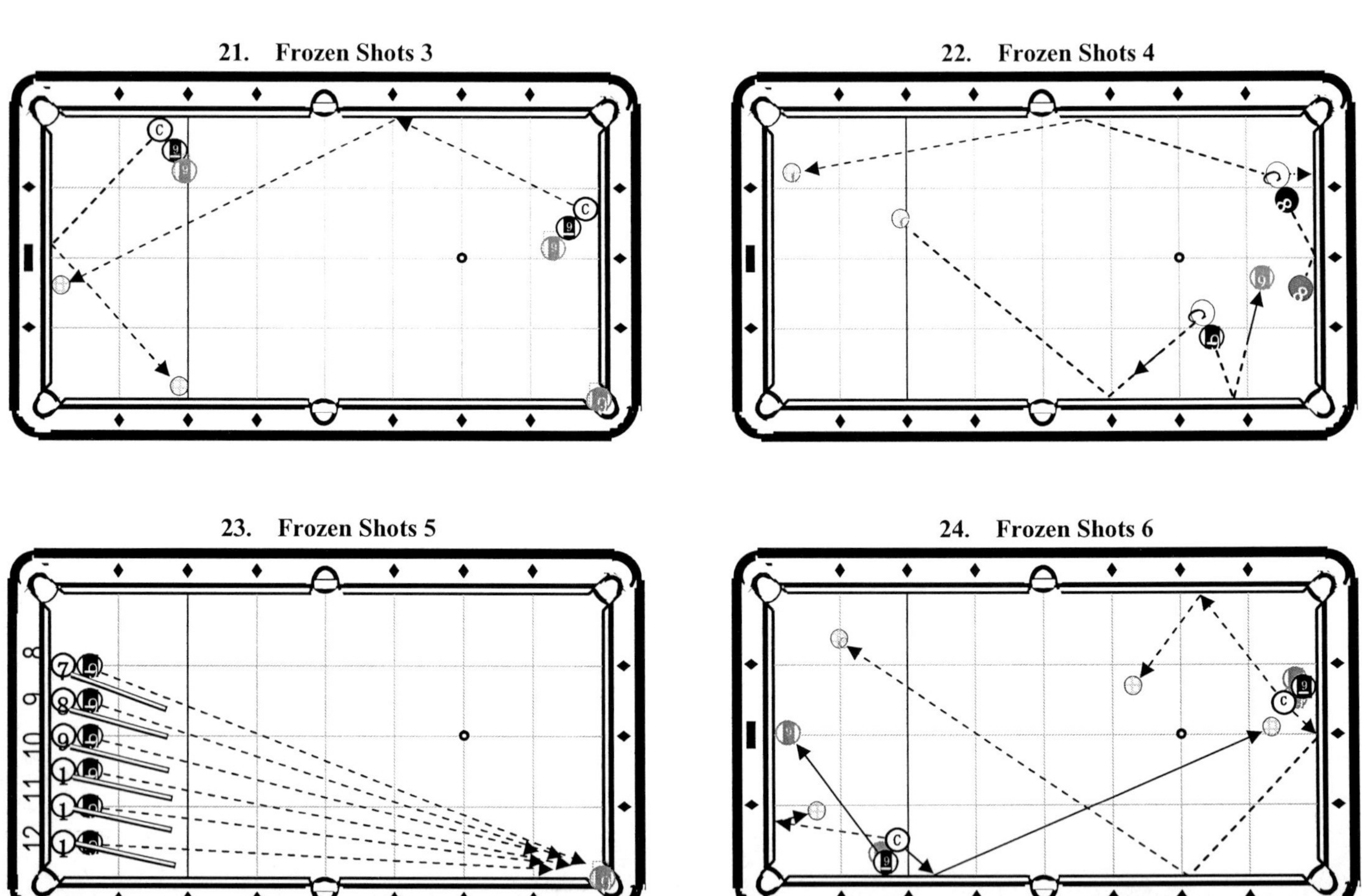
21. Frozen Shots 3
22. Frozen Shots 4
23. Frozen Shots 5
8
9
10
11
12
24. Frozen Shots 6

25. Frozen Shots 7

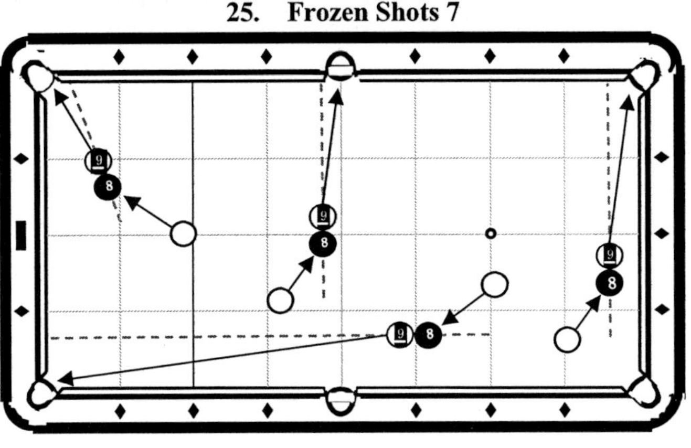

26. Frozen Shots 8

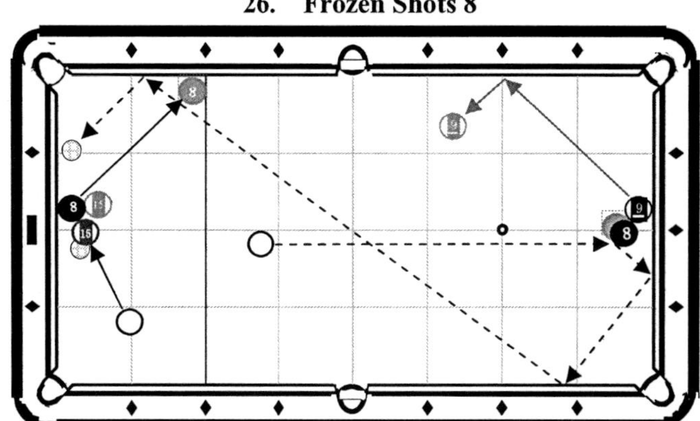

27. Jump With Your Playing Cue 101

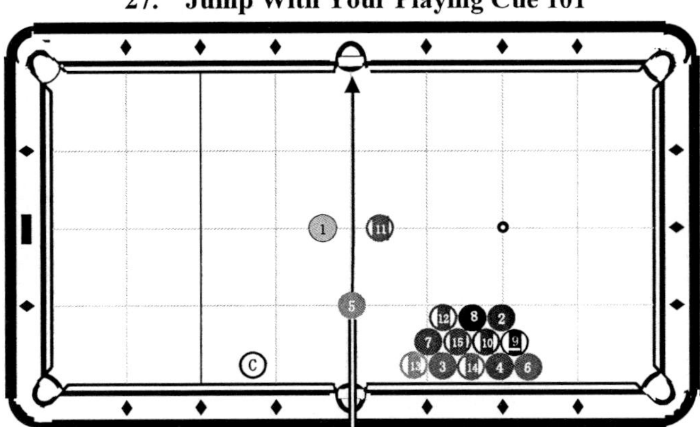

28. Jump With Your Playing Cue 102

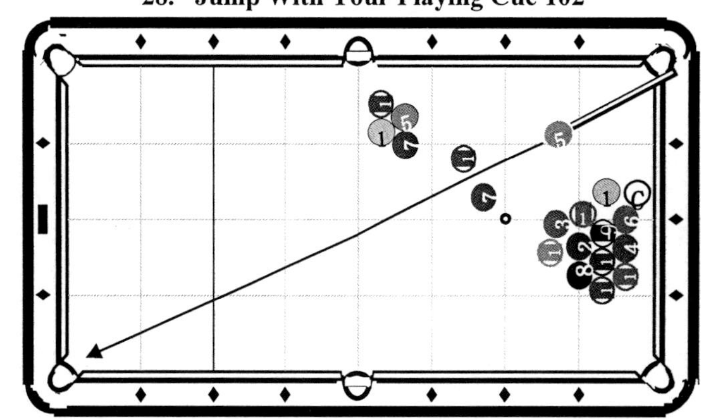

29. Massé Full Table Length

30. Massé Half Table Length

31. Massé Bank Half Table

32. Massé Bank Full Table

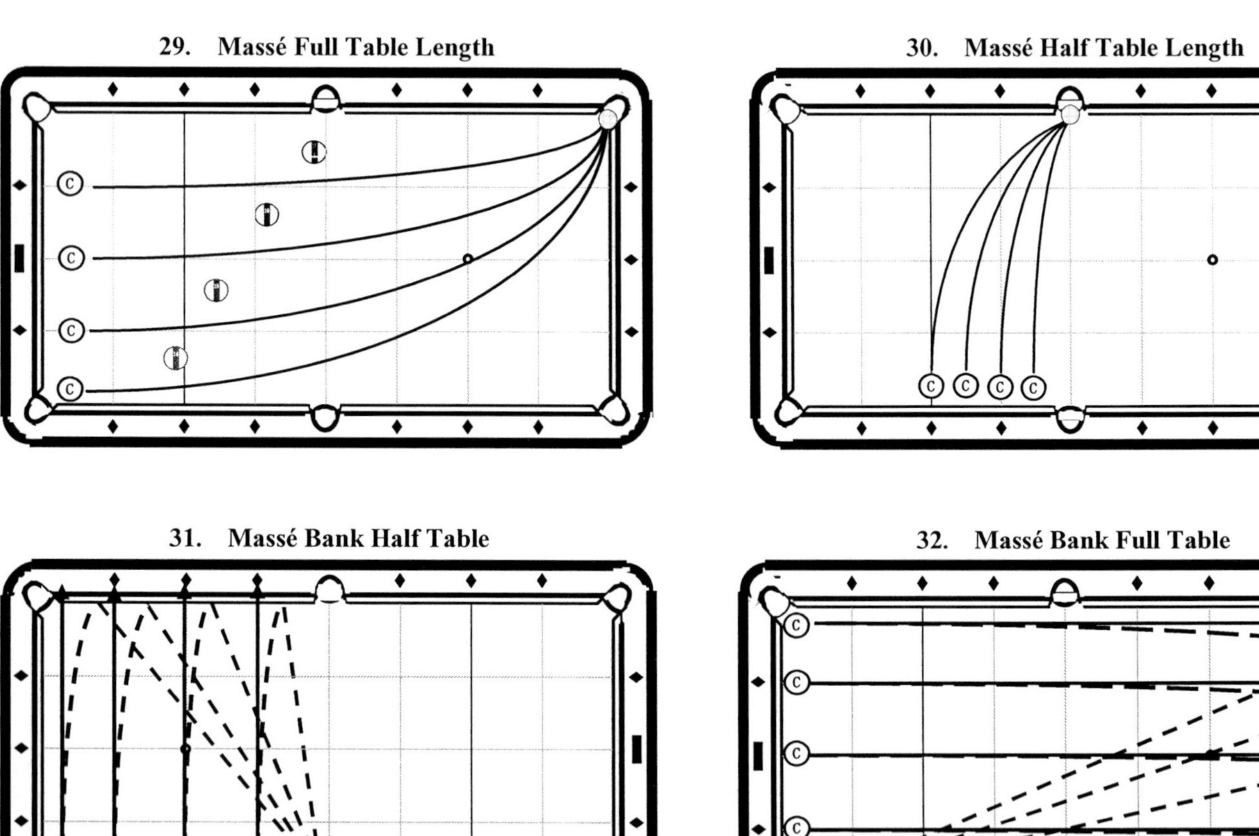

33. Double Back Bank Shot

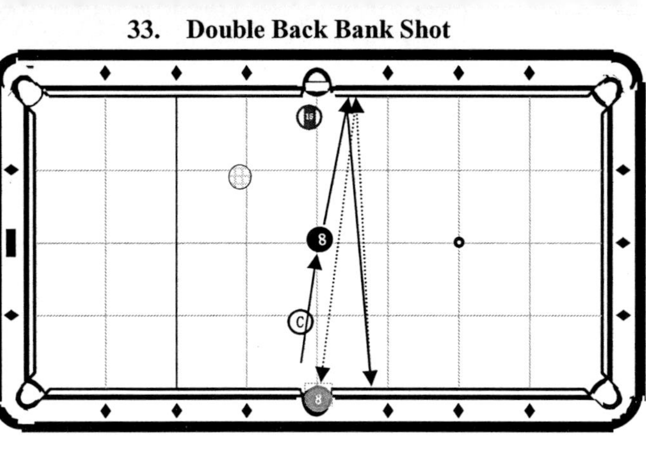

34. Frozen Inside The Pocket

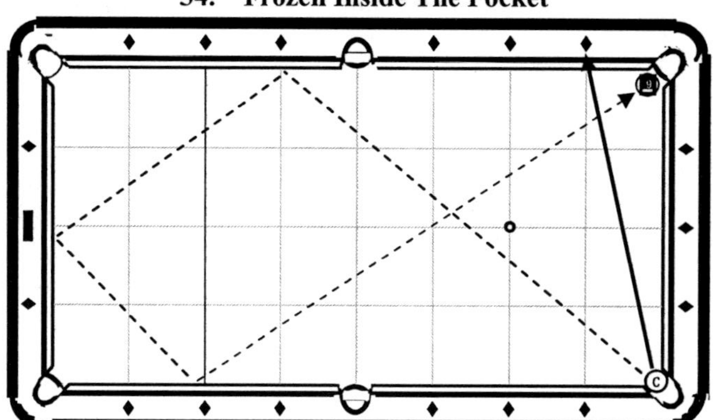

35. NOT Frozen Inside The Pocket

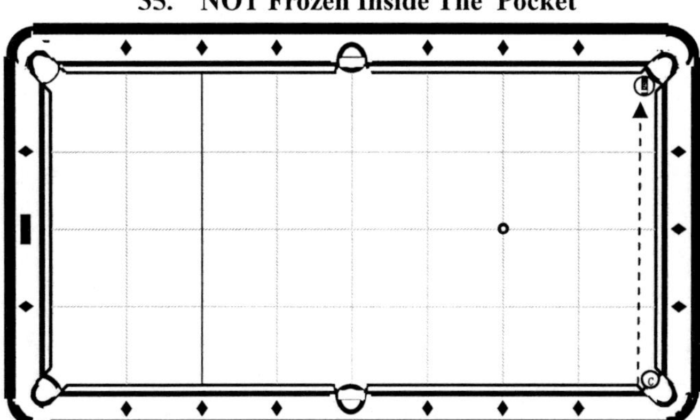

36. Frozen Shots 9

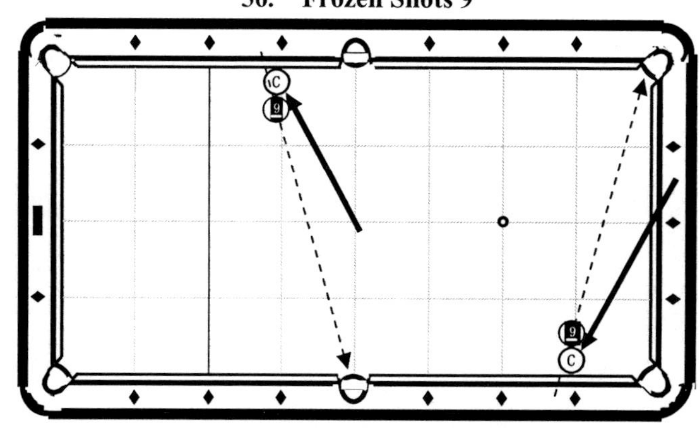

37. Object Ball In The Jaw Inside

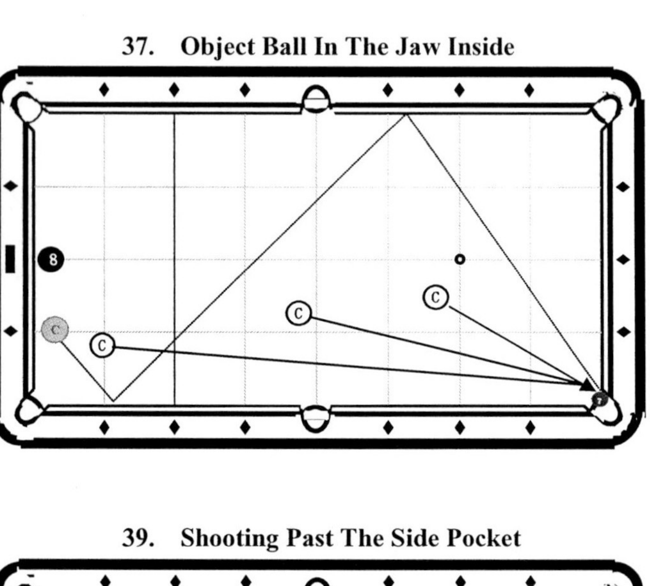

38. Object Ball In The Jaw Outside

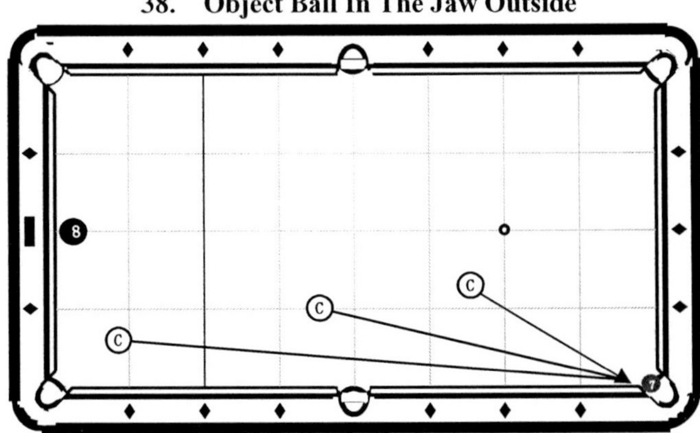

39. Shooting Past The Side Pocket

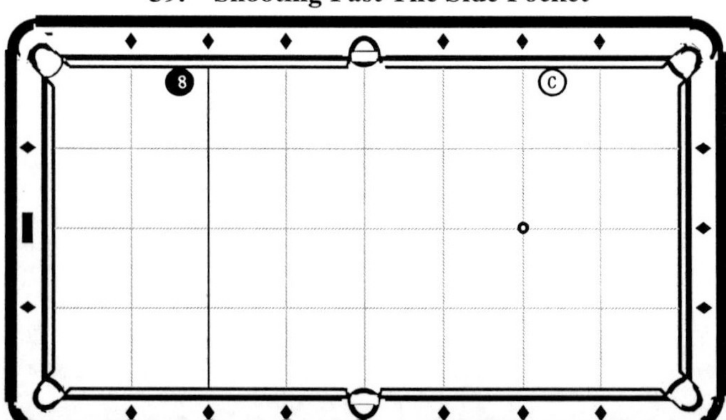

40. The 90° Rule

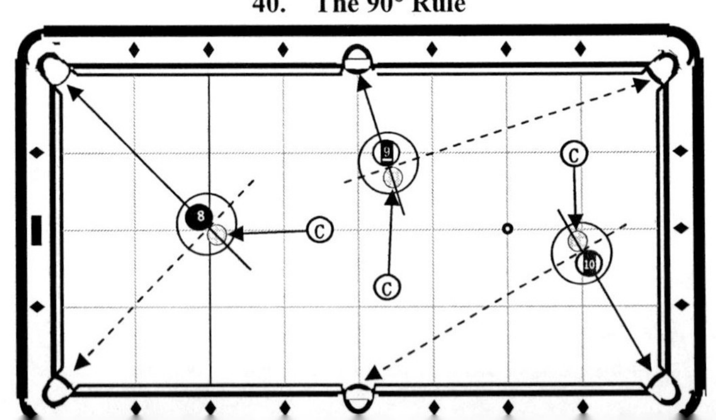

41. The 30° Rule

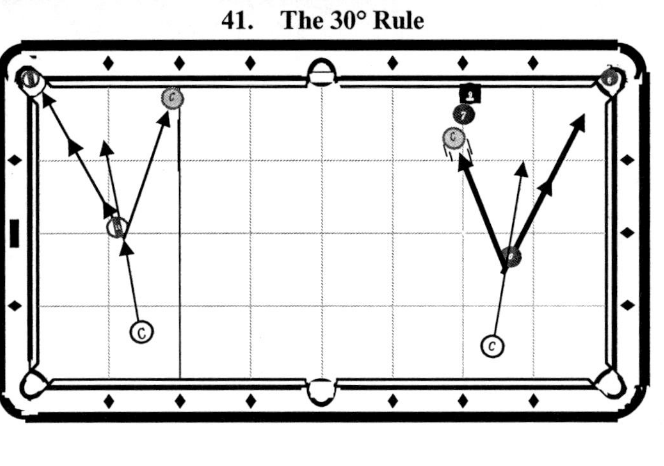

42. Frozen Rail Side Kick Shots

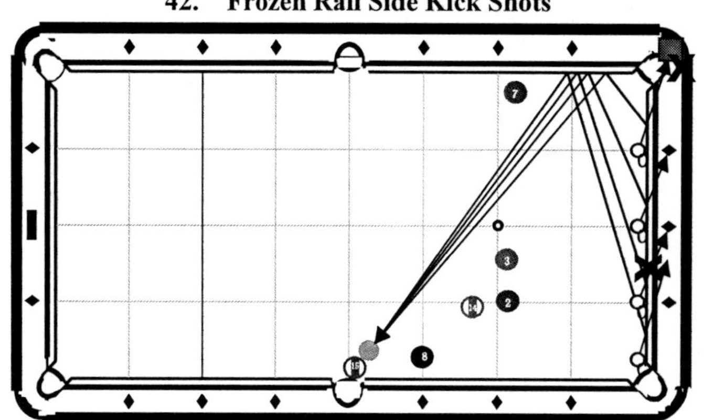

43. 3 Rail Diamond System

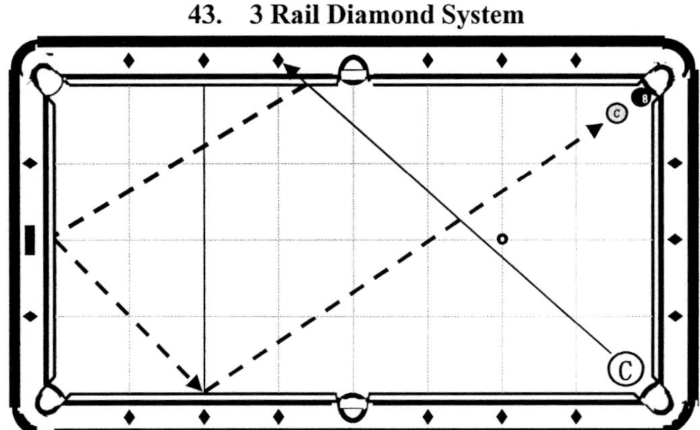

44. 4 Rail Diamond System

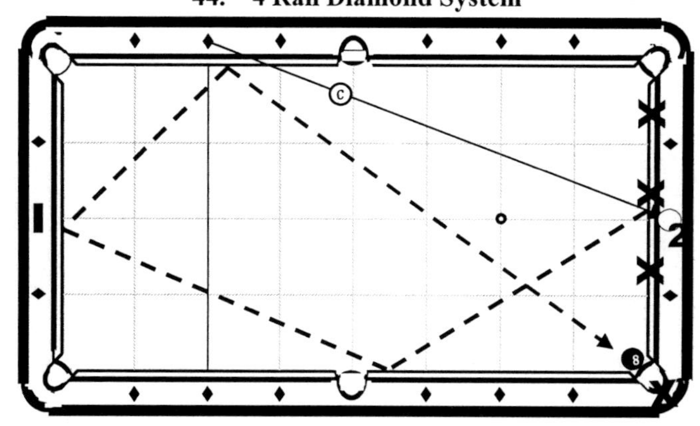

45. 5 Rail Diamond System

46. Carom Follow Shot 1

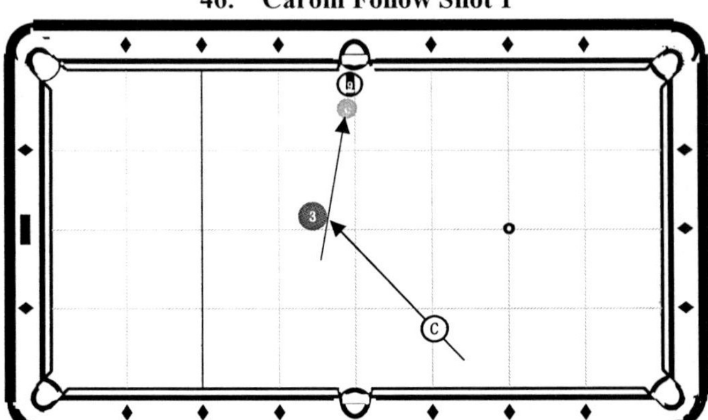

47. Carom Follow Shot 2

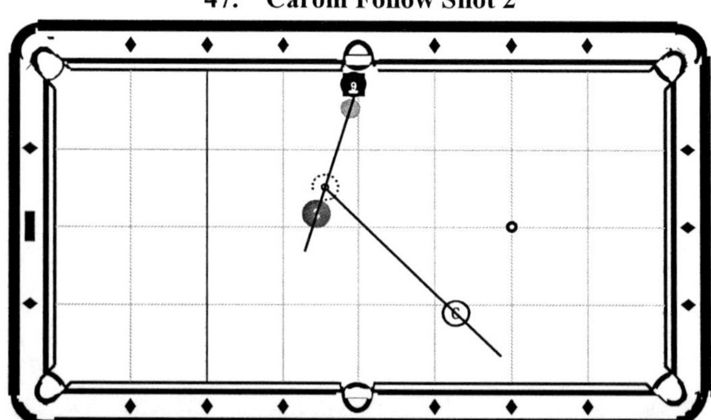

48. Carom Curve Follow Shot

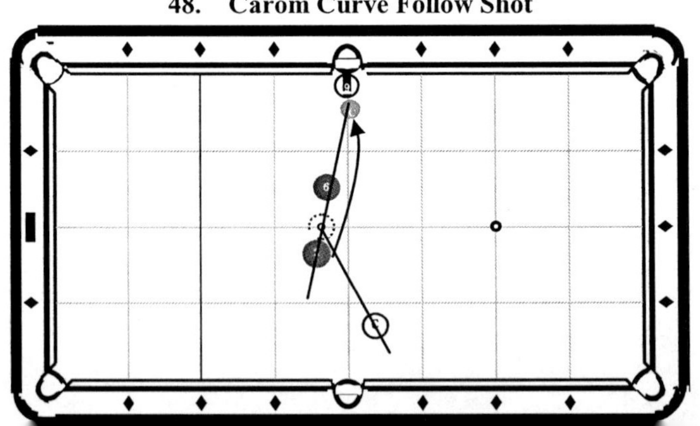

49. Carom Draw Shot

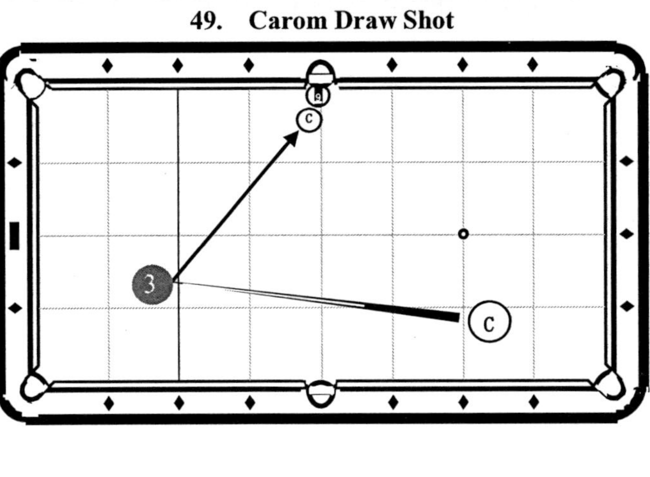

50. Across and Back Up Draw Shot

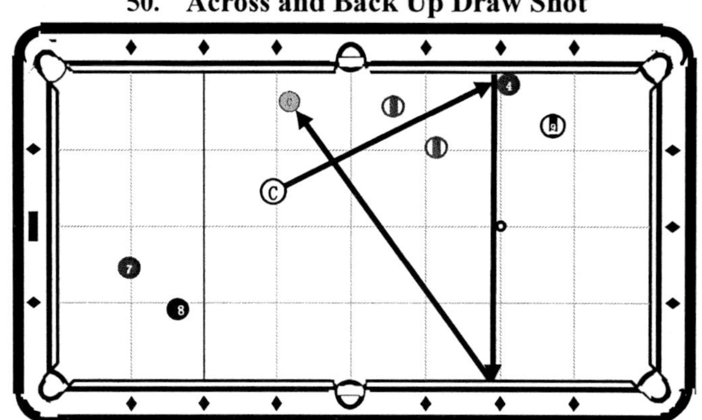

51. Passing The Hard Shot Back 1

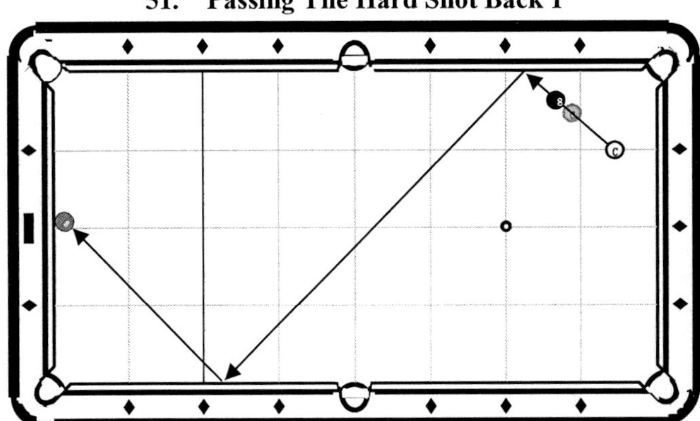

52. Passing The Hard Shot Back 2

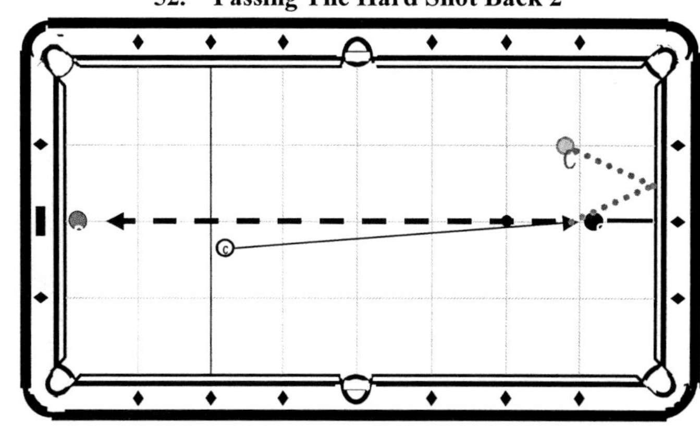

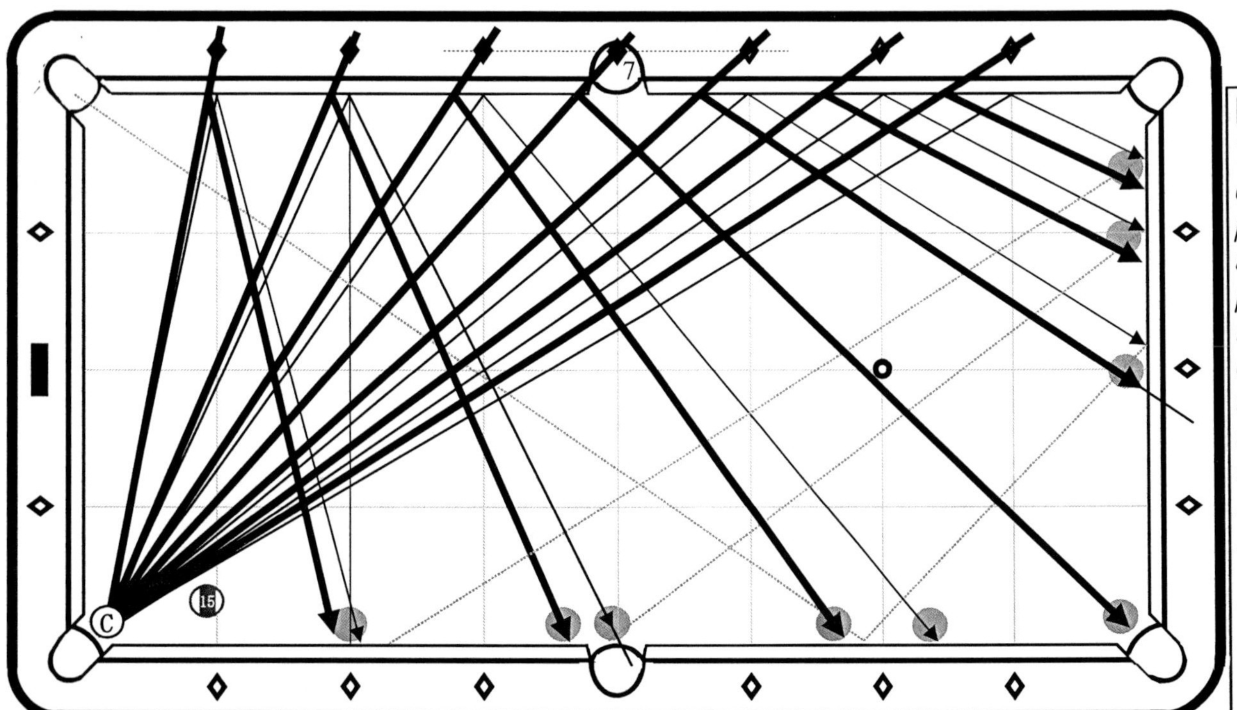

1

Foot Notes

The cue ball track can be from the pocket to almost any point on that pocket track. Natural role is best caused by stroking the cue ball above center with a level cue, a 3 to 5 Speed Stroke with a smooth release.

Don't poke the stroke!

Advanced Option ***The cue ball is blocked by the 15 ball (above):***

1. You can shorten the DTP ½ to 1 ball by using a 7 to 9 Speed Stroke with 1 to 3 Tips of Follow.
2. You can shorten the DTP up to 2 Diamonds using a 5 to 8 Speed Stroke with 1 to 3 Tips of Draw.

PROBLEM:
1. The cue ball is in the jaw of the pocket.
2. You must kick one rail to hit your object ball.
3. Applying English may cause Massé .
4. The cue ball is too close to the pocket to apply any Running or Soft English.

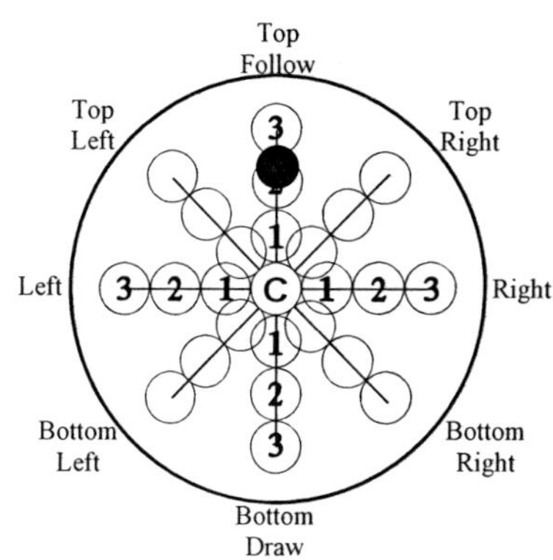

BASIC:
1. Keep your cue level through the stroke.
2. Apply ½ Tip of English above Center ball.
3. Use a 4 to 5 Speed Stroke.

ADVANCED:
1. Alter DTP aim point to affect angle out.
2. Elevated butt shortens angle out.
3. Draw shortens angle out.
4. Slower speed enhances angle out.

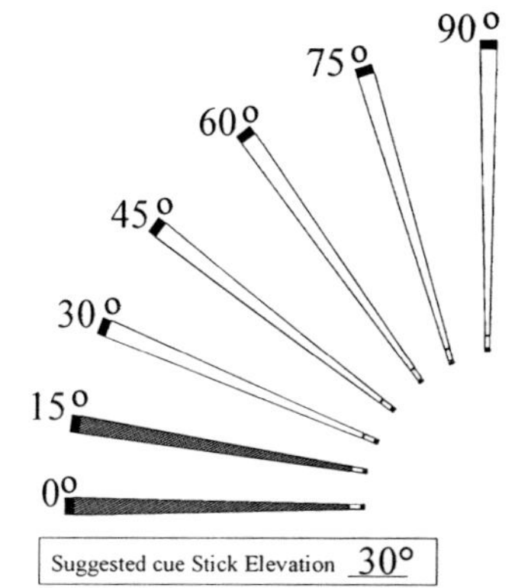

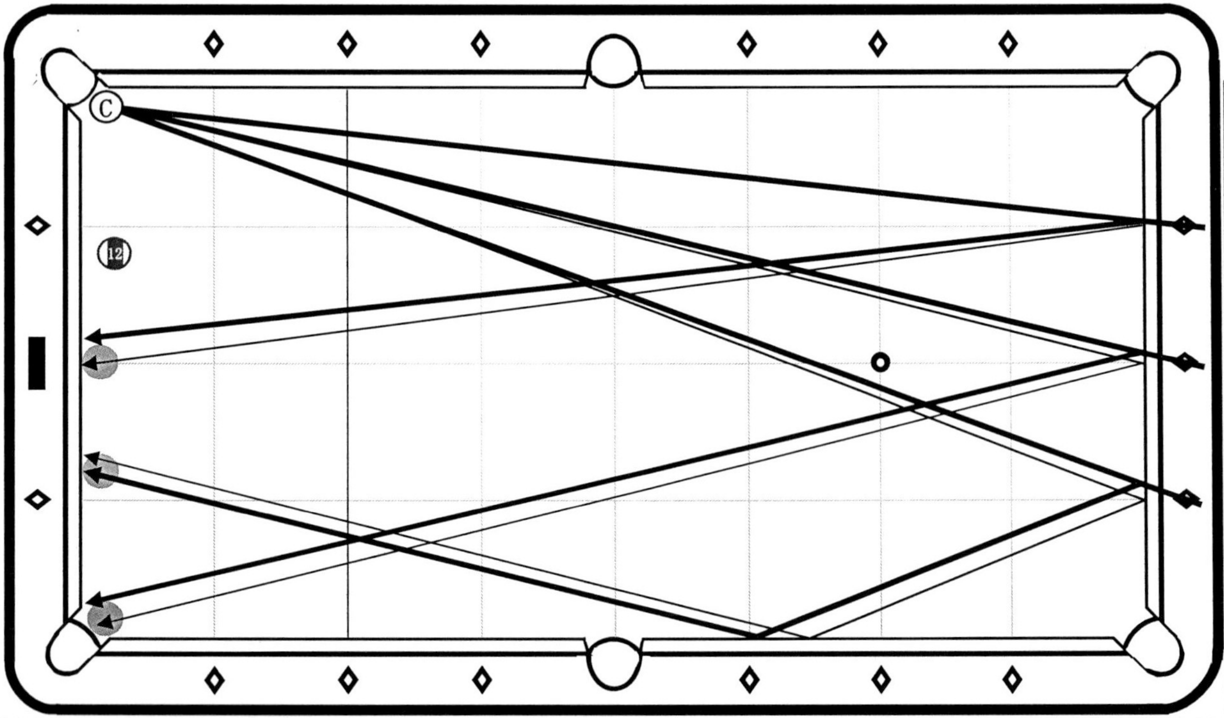

C

12

Foot Notes

The cue ball track can be from the pocket to almost any point on that pocket track. Natural role is best caused by stroking the cue ball above center with a level cue, a 3 to 5 Speed ***smooth*** *Stroke release.*

Don't poke the stroke!

Advanced Option ***The cue ball is blocked by the 12 ball (above):***

1. Jump the 12 Ball with a jump cue.
2. To pocket corner ball, Massé (Aim 1 Diamond out, Jack Up 45°, 2 Tips Inside, 5 Speed Stroke).

PROBLEM: 1. The cue ball is in the jaw of the pocket.
2. You must kick one rail to hit your object ball.
3. Applying English may cause Massé .
4. The cue ball is too close to the pocket to apply any Running or Soft English.

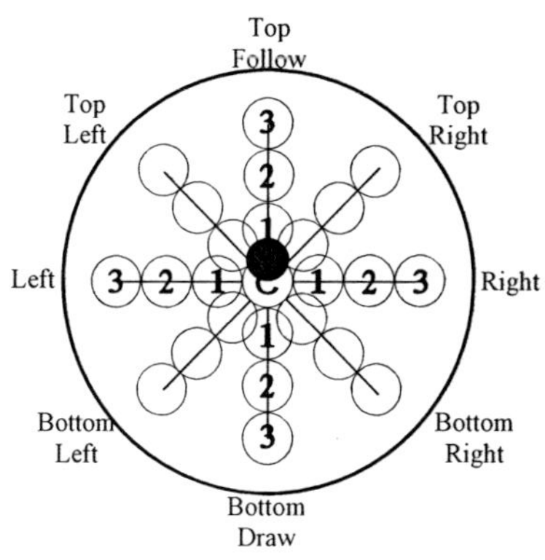

BASIC:

1. Keep your cue level through the stroke.
2. Apply ½ Tip of English above Center Ball.
3. Use a 5 to 6 Speed Stroke.

ADVANCED:

1. Alter DTP aim points to affect angle out.
2. Jump
3. Massé

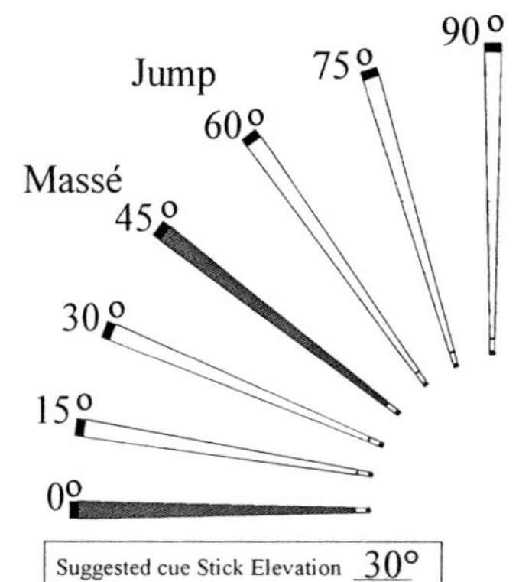

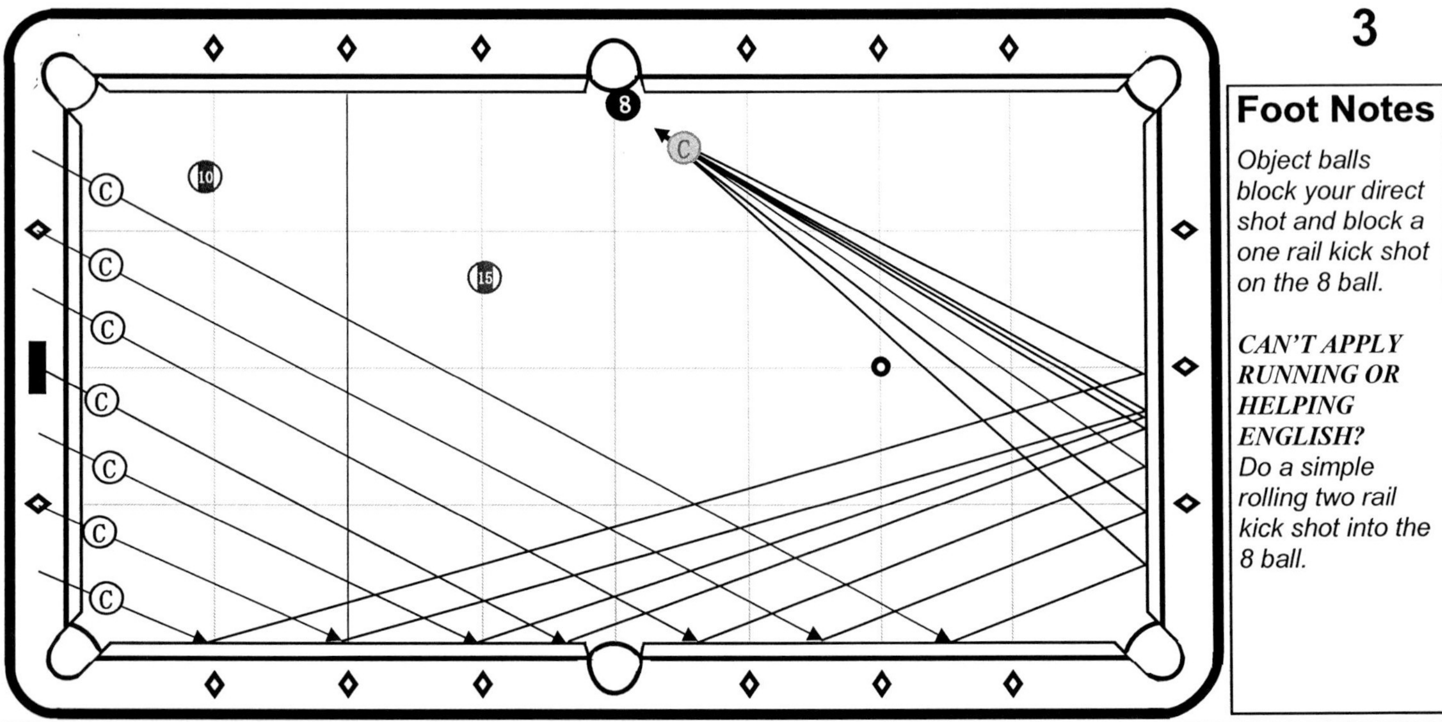

Foot Notes

Object balls block your direct shot and block a one rail kick shot on the 8 ball.

CAN'T APPLY RUNNING OR HELPING ENGLISH?
Do a simple rolling two rail kick shot into the 8 ball.

Advanced Option ***The cue ball is blocked by the 10 ball (above):***

1. Jump the 10 Ball with a jump cue.
2. Massé around 10 Ball (Aim 1 Diamond out, Jack Up 45°, 2 Tips Inside, 5 Speed Stroke).
3. Shoot into 3rd Diamond of side rail, cue Up 30°, 2+ Tips outside English, 7 Speed Stroke.

PROBLEM: 1. The cue ball is blocked for a straight in shot.
2. The 15 ball blocks a one rail kick shot.
3. You must kick two rails to hit the 8 ball.
4. The cue ball is too close to the rail to apply any Running or Soft English.

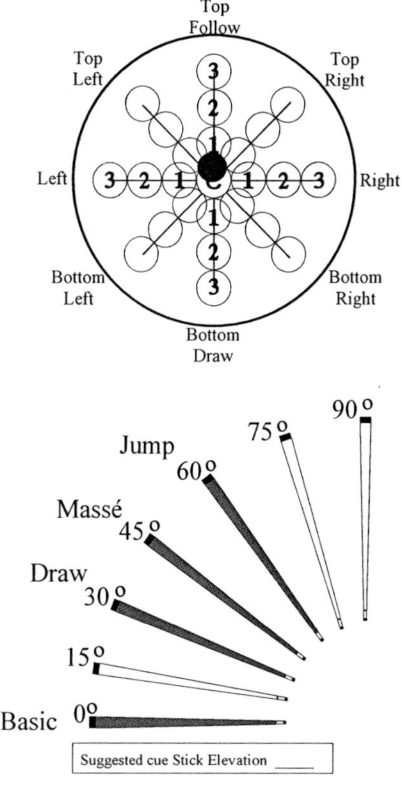

BASIC:

1. Keep your cue level through the stroke.
2. Apply ½ Tip English above Center Ball.
3. Use a 4 Speed Stroke.
4. Aim at the DTP with NO English (SPIN).

ADVANCED:

1. Jump
2. Massé
3. Kick into the 3rd Diamond, Jack Up 30°, 3 Tips of Bottom Right, and a 6 Speed Stroke.

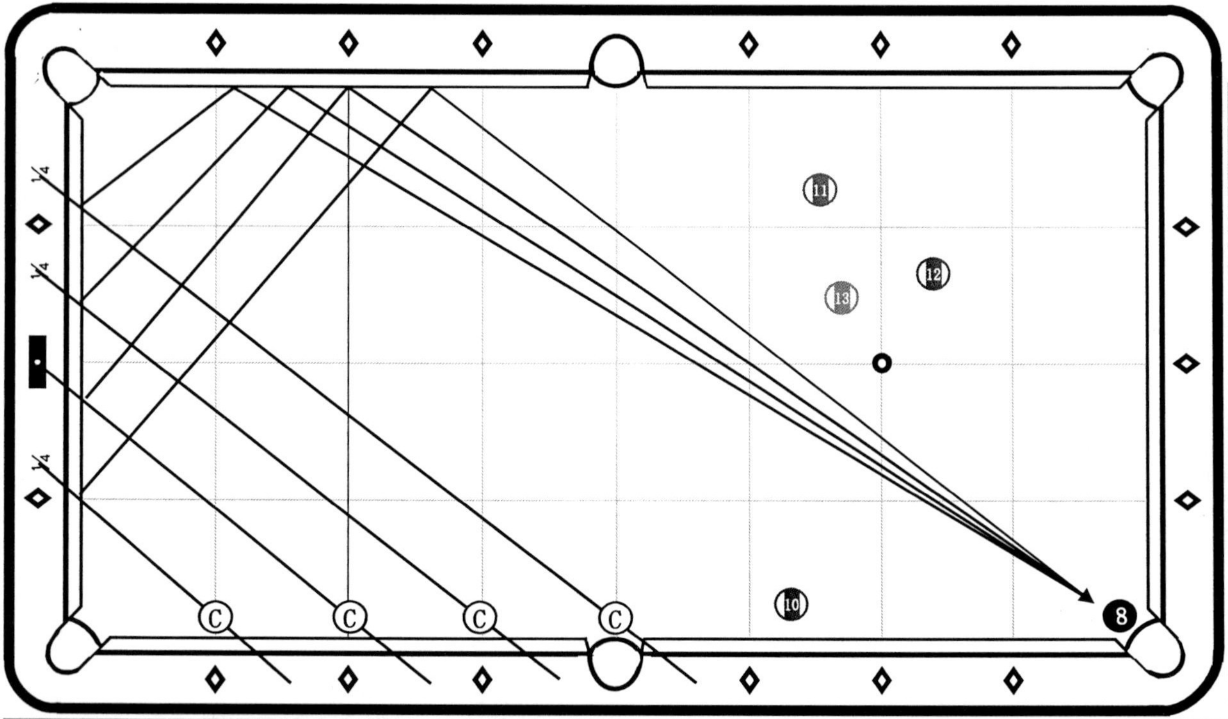

Foot Notes

Object balls block your direct shot and block a one rail kick shot on the 8 ball.

CAN'T APPLY RUNNING OR HELPING ENGLISH?
Do a simple rolling two rail kick shot into the 8 ball.

Advanced Option ***The cue ball is blocked by the 10 ball (above):***

1. Jump the 10 Ball with a jump cue.
2. Massé around 10 Ball (Aim 1 Diamond out, Jack Up 45°, 2 Tips Inside, 5 Speed Stroke).

PROBLEM:
1. The cue ball is blocked for a straight in shot.
2. Object balls block a one rail kick shot.
3. You must kick two rails to hit the 8 ball.
4. The cue ball is too close to the rail to apply any Running or Soft English.

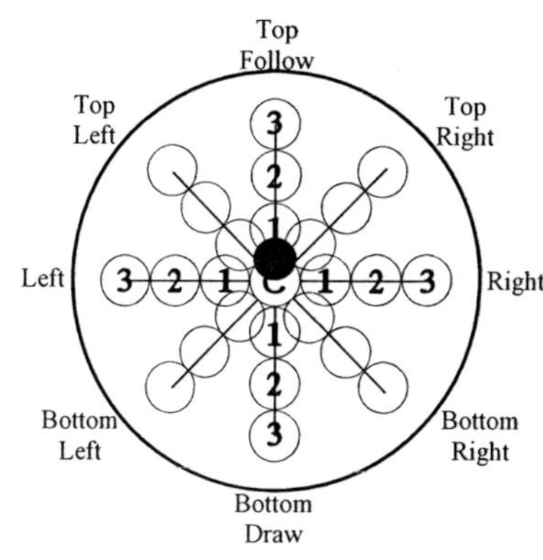

BASIC:
1. Keep your cue level through the stroke.
2. Apply ½ Tip English above Center Ball.
3. Use a 4 Speed Stroke.
4. Aim at the DTP with NO English (SPIN).

ADVANCED:
1. Jump
2. Massé

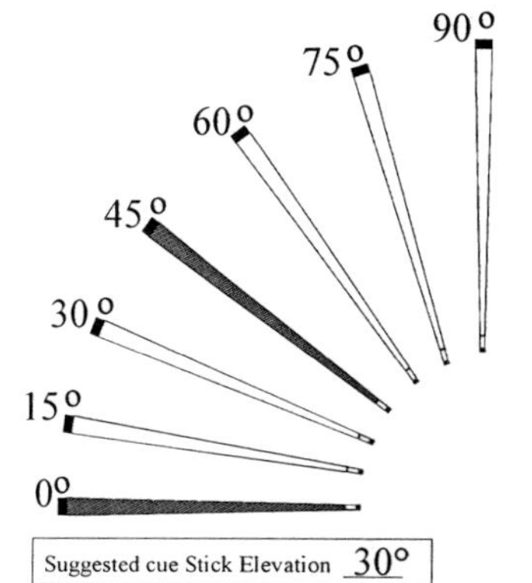

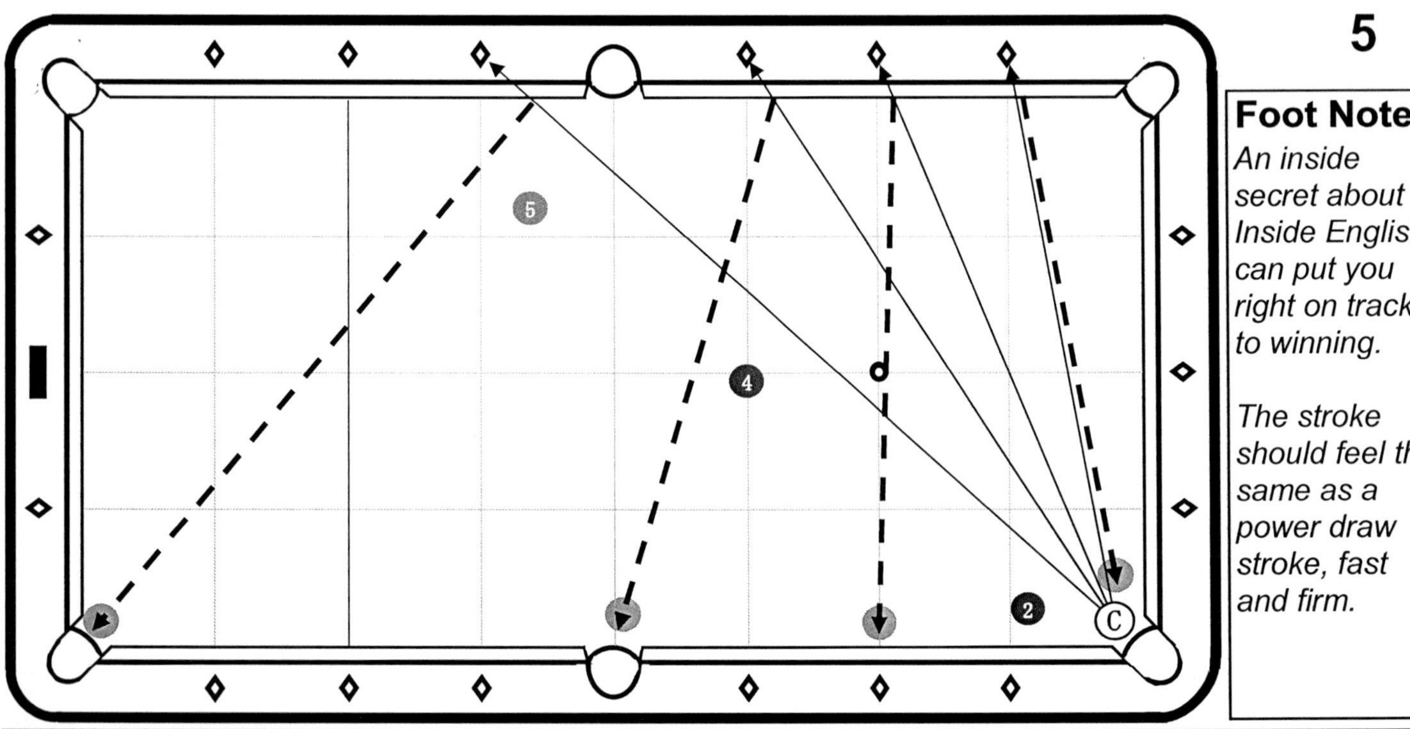

Foot Notes

An inside secret about Inside English can put you right on track to winning.

The stroke should feel the same as a power draw stroke, fast and firm.

Advanced Option

Altered cue elevations and speeds can shorten or lengthen these cue ball paths.

PROBLEM: 1. The cue ball is blocked for a straight in shot.
2. Object balls block a natural roll kick shot.

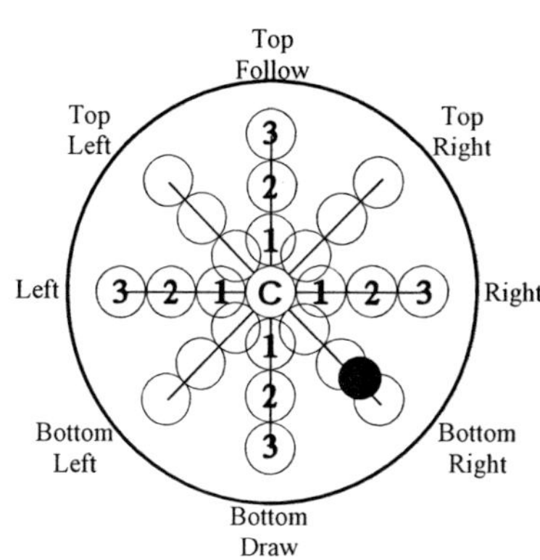

BASIC:

1. Learn the Diamond Contact Points (DCP) by heart.
2. Use 4:30 Bottom Inside English.
3. Elevate Butt of Cue Stick 15° to 30°.
4. Use 5 to 7 Speed Stroke.
5. Apply a smooth follow-through stroke.

ADVANCED:

1. Alter Butt Elevations.
2. Change Stroke Speeds.

NOTE:

Use this Inside English shot to shorten the cue ball path when an object ball obstructs the standard kicking angles.

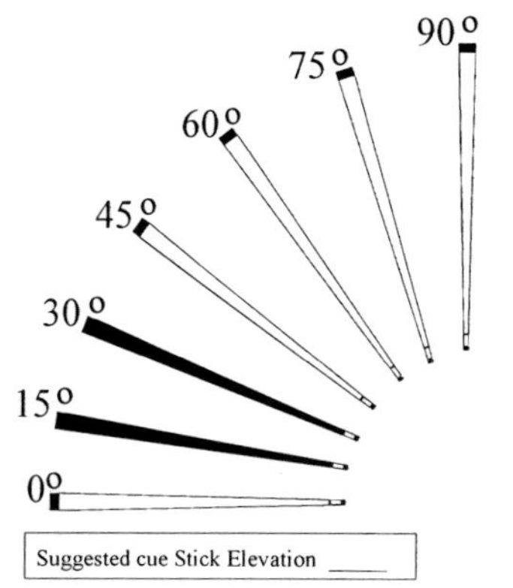

5 SHORT RAIL KICK - INSIDE ENGLISH

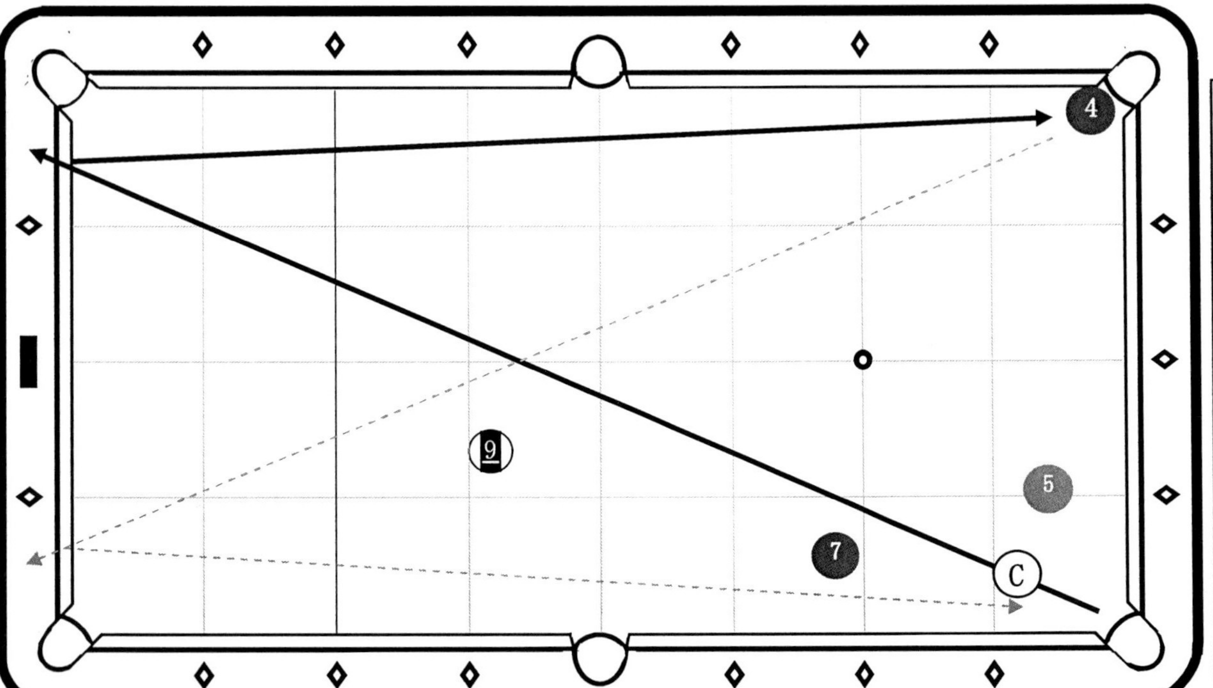

Foot Notes

The use of an Inside English shot like this is due to odd cue ball path obstructions that won't allow more standard kicking angles to work well. That makes these shots all the more important to know.

Advanced Option

Altered cue elevation and speed can shorten or lengthen these cue ball paths based on how the table is playing.

PROBLEM:

1. Cue ball is blocked by the 5 ball for a straight in shot on the 4 ball.
2. Object balls block a natural roll kick shot.

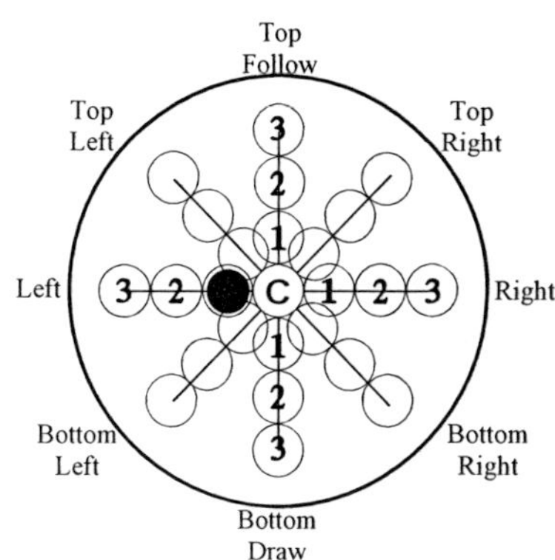

BASIC:

1. Learn the Diamond Contact Point (DCP) by heart.
2. Use 1 Tip Inside English.
3. Level cue stick elevation.
4. Use a 5 to 7 Speed Stroke.
5. Apply a smooth follow-through stroke.

ADVANCED: You can also play the 4 ball by:

1. Jump
2. Massé

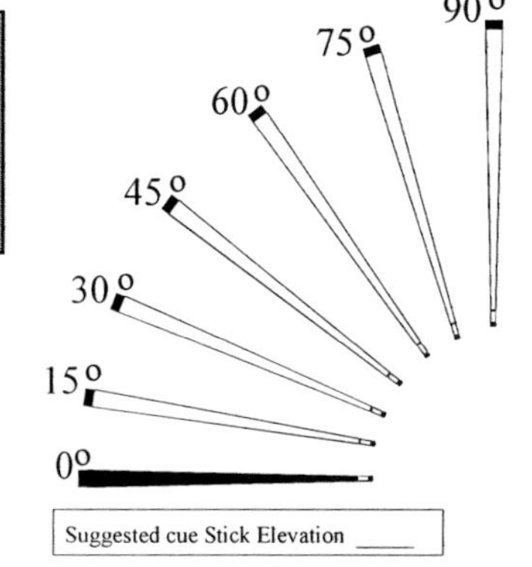

6 1 RAIL KICK - INSIDE ENGLISH

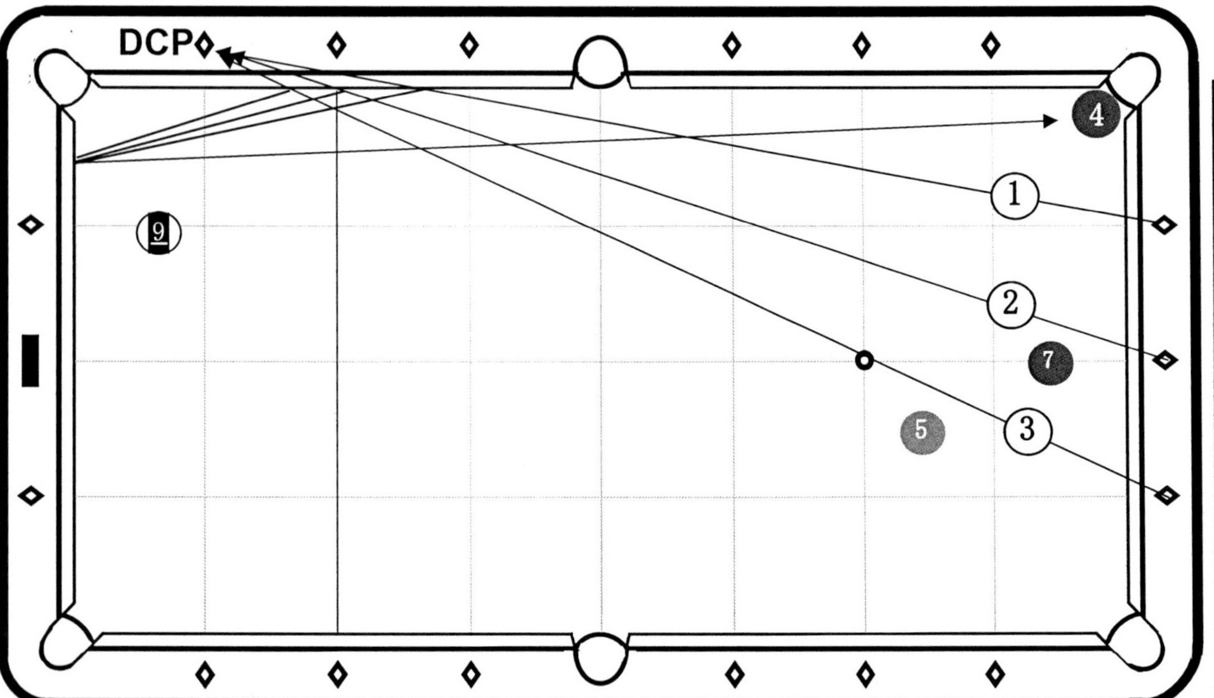

Foot Notes

The use of an Inside English shot like this is due to odd cue ball path obstructions that won't allow more standard kicking angles to work well. That makes these shots all the more important to know.

Advanced Option

Altered cue elevation and speed can shorten or lengthen these cue ball paths based on how the table is playing.

PROBLEM:

1. Cue ball is blocked by the 7 ball for a straight in shot on the 4 ball.
2. Other object balls block a natural roll kick shot.

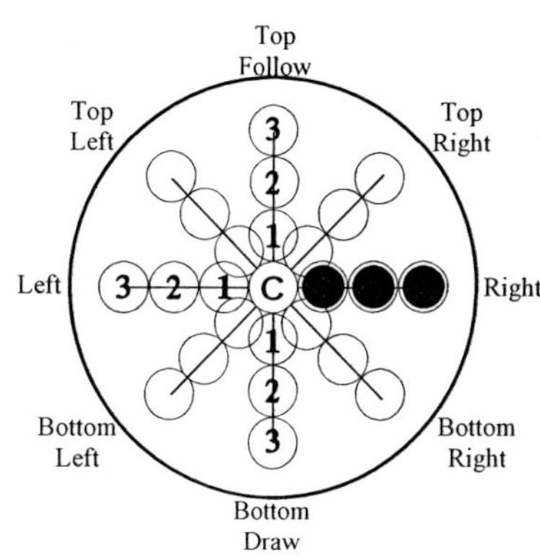

BASIC:

1. Learn the Diamond Contact Point (DCP) by heart.
2. Use 1 Tip of Inside English from 1 Diamond out. (1)
3. Use 2 Tips of Inside English from 2 Diamonds out. (2)
4. Use 3 Tips of Inside English from 3 Diamonds out. (3)
5. Level cue stick elevation.
6. Use a 5 to 6 Speed Stroke.
7. Apply a smooth follow-through stroke.

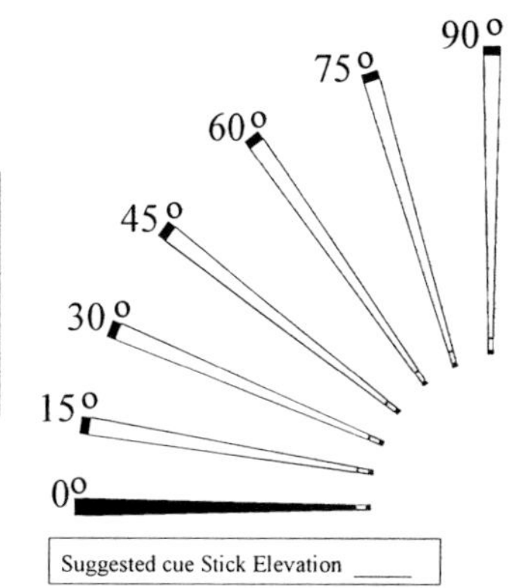

ADVANCED: You can also play the 4 ball by:

1. Jump
2. Massé

7 2 RAIL KICK - INSIDE ENGLISH

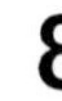

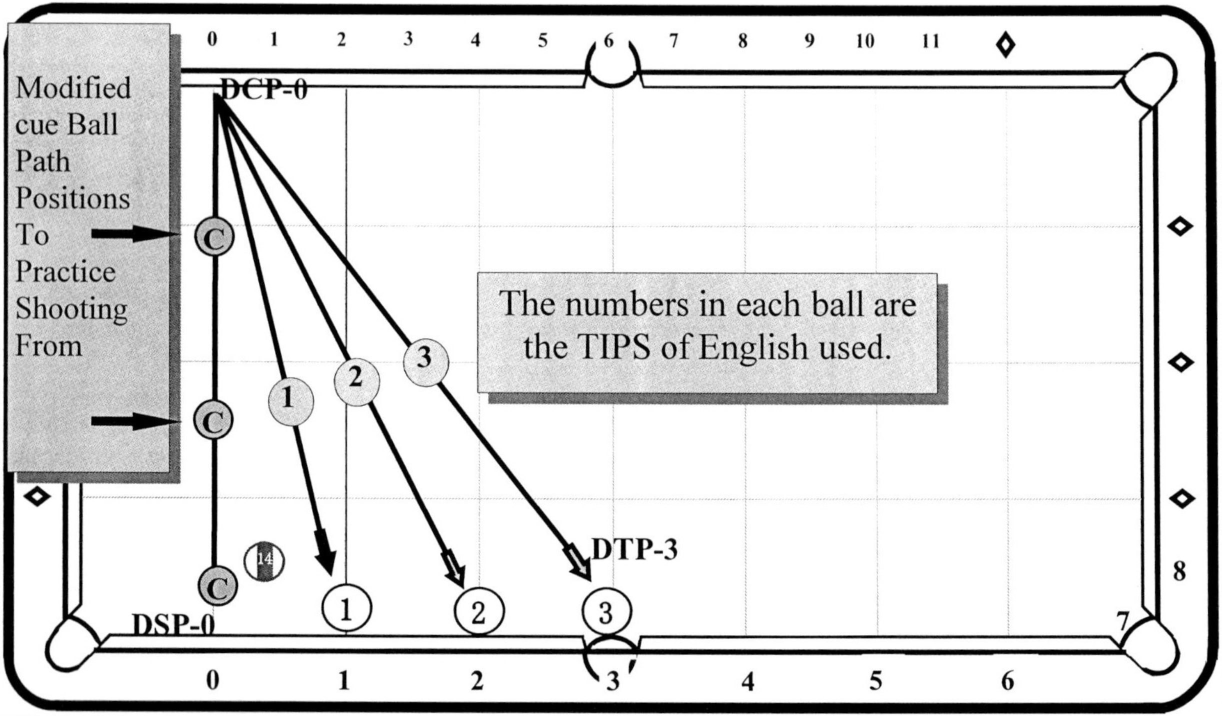
0 1 2 3 4 5 6 7 8 9 10 11
DCP-0
Modified cue Ball Path Positions To Practice Shooting From
C
C
C
14
1
2
3
The numbers in each ball are the TIPS of English used.
DTP-3
1
2
3
DSP-0
8
7
0 1 2 3 4 5 6

Foot Notes

Throughout Pro Skill Drills, I often advise to use 1, 2, or 3 Tips of English (SPIN). In this exercise and throughout, I use a 4 to 6 Speed Stroke, which results in reaching the DTP of 1, 2, or 3 Diamonds.

Slower or faster speeds will affect the angle out of the rail and you should test these.

Advanced Option

Altering speeds can shorten or lengthen these cue ball paths.

PROBLEM: 1. Cue ball is blocked for a straight in shot.
2. Object ball blocks a natural roll kick shot.

BASIC:

1. Place the cue ball in front of **Diamond Starting Point 0 (DSP)**, about 4 to 6 inches off the rail.
2. Place an object ball on the rail at **Diamond Target Points (DTP)** 1, 2, & 3, as shown above.
3. Shoot with 1-Tip English Right of Center on the cue ball into **Diamond Contact Point 0 (DCP)** to hit the 1 ball.
4. Shoot with 2-Tips English Right of Center on the cue ball into **DCP-0** to hit the 2 ball.
5. Shoot with 3-Tips English Right of Center on the cue ball into **DCP-0** to hit the 3 ball.

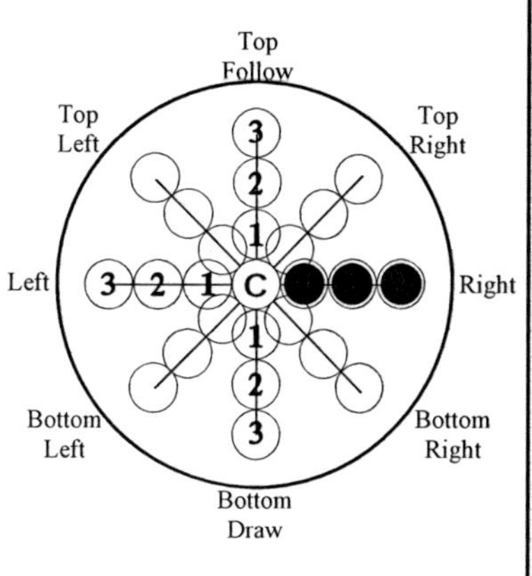

ADVANCED:

1. Stroke Speed can shorten or lengthen the DTP.

NOTE: Shoot for each Diamond position many times to ingrain the feel of your stroke and you'll master pin point cue ball path accuracy. This drill will pay off many times over.

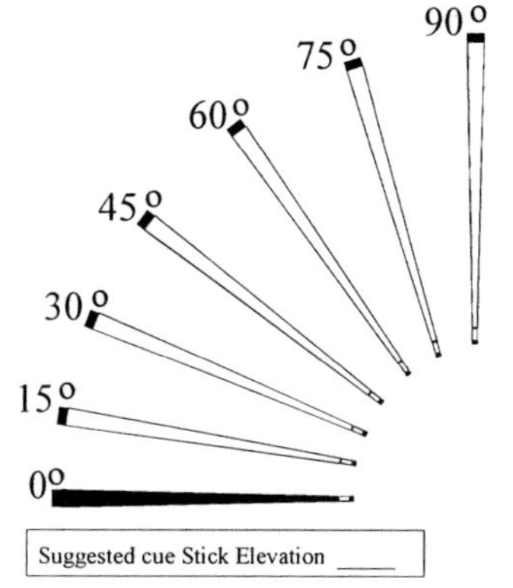

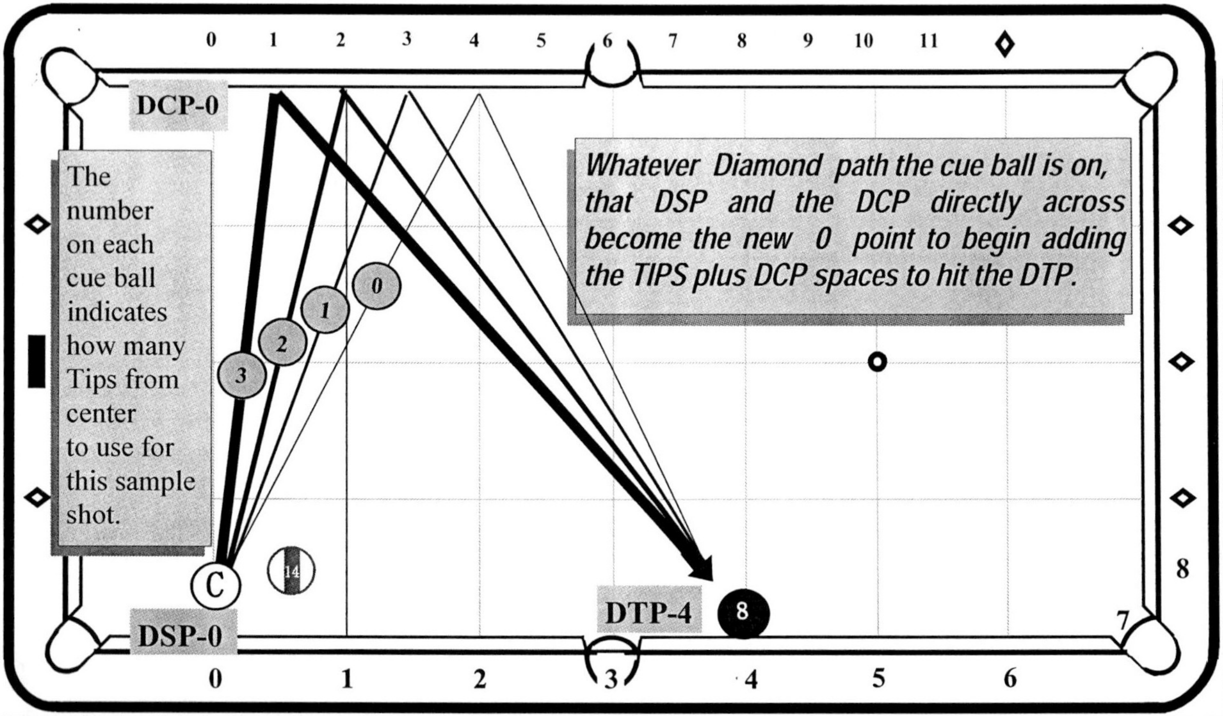

0 1 2 3 4 5 6 7 8 9 10 11

DCP-0

The number on each cue ball indicates how many Tips from center to use for this sample shot.

Whatever Diamond path the cue ball is on, that DSP and the DCP directly across become the new 0 point to begin adding the TIPS plus DCP spaces to hit the DTP.

0 1 2 3 C 14 8

DSP-0 DTP-4

0 1 2 3 4 5 6 7 8

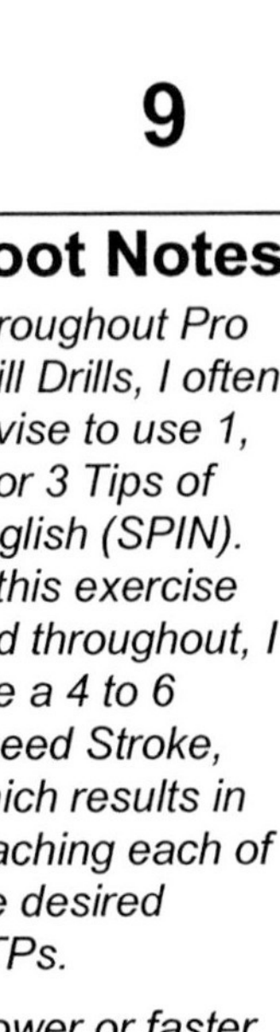

Foot Notes

Throughout Pro Skill Drills, I often advise to use 1, 2, or 3 Tips of English (SPIN). In this exercise and throughout, I use a 4 to 6 Speed Stroke, which results in reaching each of the desired DTPs.

Slower or faster speeds will affect the angle out of the rail and you should test these.

Advanced Option

Altering speeds can shorten or lengthen these cue ball paths.

PROBLEM: 1. Object ball blocks a natural roll kick shot.

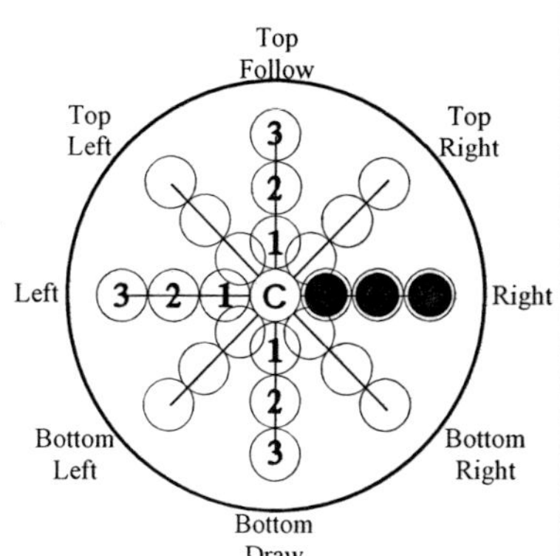

BASIC Starting Explanation:

A.) Diamonds 1-8 on the bottom long rail are the **DSP: Diamond Start Point**.
B.) Diamonds 1-11 on the top long rail are the **DCP: Diamond Contact Point**.
C.) The 8 ball is located at the **DTP: Target Diamond Starting Point**.
D.) The gray cue balls show the number of TIPS of English to use (see the English Striking Point diagram below).

1. Place the cue ball in front of **(DSP) 0**, about 6 inches off the rail (the cue ball can be shot from almost any point on that DSP cue ball track).
2 Place the 8 ball on the rail at **DTP-4 (Four Diamonds up the same side rail).**
3 Use 3-Tips Right English into **DCP-1**, to hit the 8 ball at **DTP 4.**
4 Use 2-Tips Right English into **DCP-2**, to hit the 8 ball at **DTP 4.**
5 Use 1-Tip Right English, into **DCP-3**, to hit the 8 ball at **DTP 4.**
6 Use Center English into **DCP-4**, to hit the 8 ball at **DTP 4.**

Q: What equals 4 Diamonds? DSP- 0 using 3 Tips + **DCP+1 = DTP 4 (3+1=4).**

ADVANCED: Count the number of Diamonds. Then starting at **DCP-0,** count down until you reach the 3, 2, 1, 0 **DCP**, then apply that number Tip of English. This way is a faster system of counting.

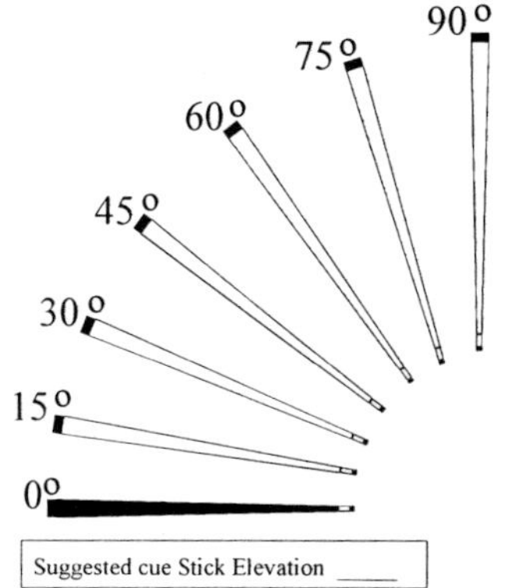

9 KICKING BY TIPS OF ENGLISH 2

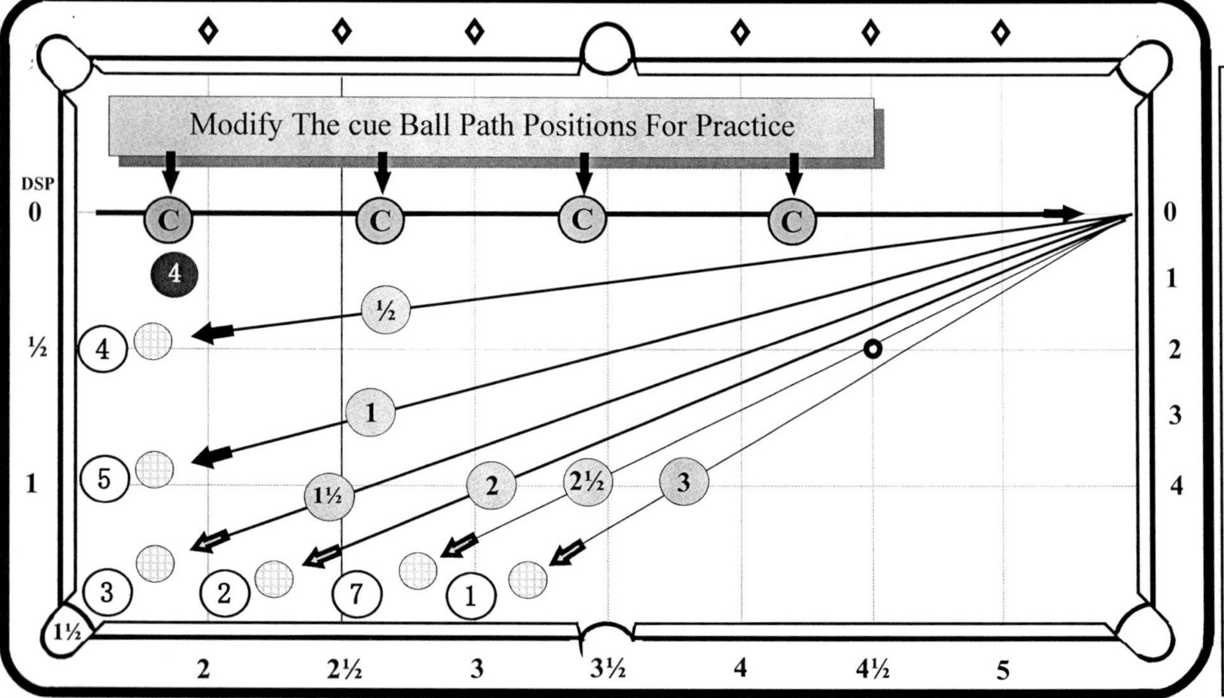

Foot Notes

Throughout Pro Skill Drills, I often advise to use 1, 2, or 3 Tips of English (SPIN). In this exercise and throughout, I use a 4 to 6 Speed Stroke, which results in reaching the DTP of ½, 1, 1½ 2, 2½, or 3 Diamonds.

Slower or faster speeds will affect the angle out of the rail and you should test these.

Advanced Option

Altering speeds can shorten or lengthen these cue ball paths.

PROBLEM: 1. Object ball blocks a natural roll kick shot.

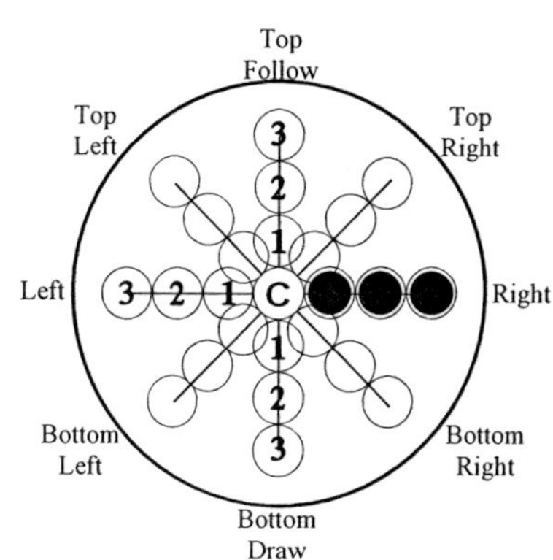

BASIC:

1. Place the cue ball in front of **DSP 0**, about 4 to 7 inches off the rail.
2. Place an object ball on the rails at each of the **DTP,** as shown above.
3. Shoot with a ½-Tip of English, into **DCP 0** to hit the 4 ball.
4. Shoot with 1-Tip of English, into **DCP 0** to hit the 5 ball.
5. Shoot with 1½-Tips of English, into **DCP 0** to pocket the 3 ball.
6. Shoot with 2-Tips of English, into **DCP 0** to hit the 2 ball.
7. Shoot with 2½-Tips of English, into **DCP 0** to hit the 7 ball.
8. Shoot with 3-Tips of English, into **DCP 0** to hit the 1 ball.

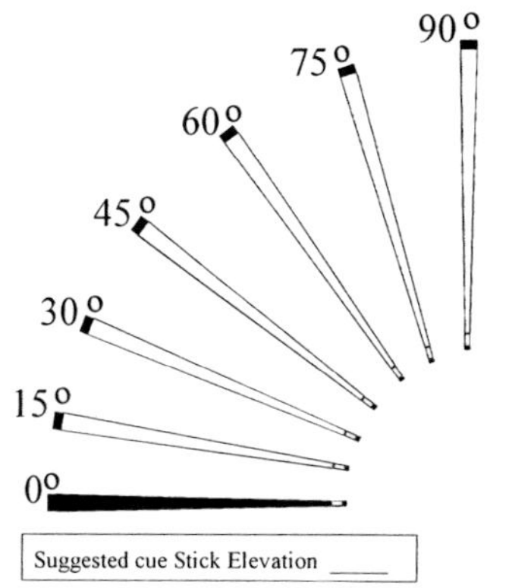

ADVANCED:

1. Continue counting **DTPs, moving up,** past the 1 ball by ½ Diamonds. Count each new **DCP (moving by** ½ Diamonds) as one whole Tip per ½ Diamond.
1. Test Shot: From **DSO-0, aim at DCP-2 + 2 Tips Right English = DTP-4.**

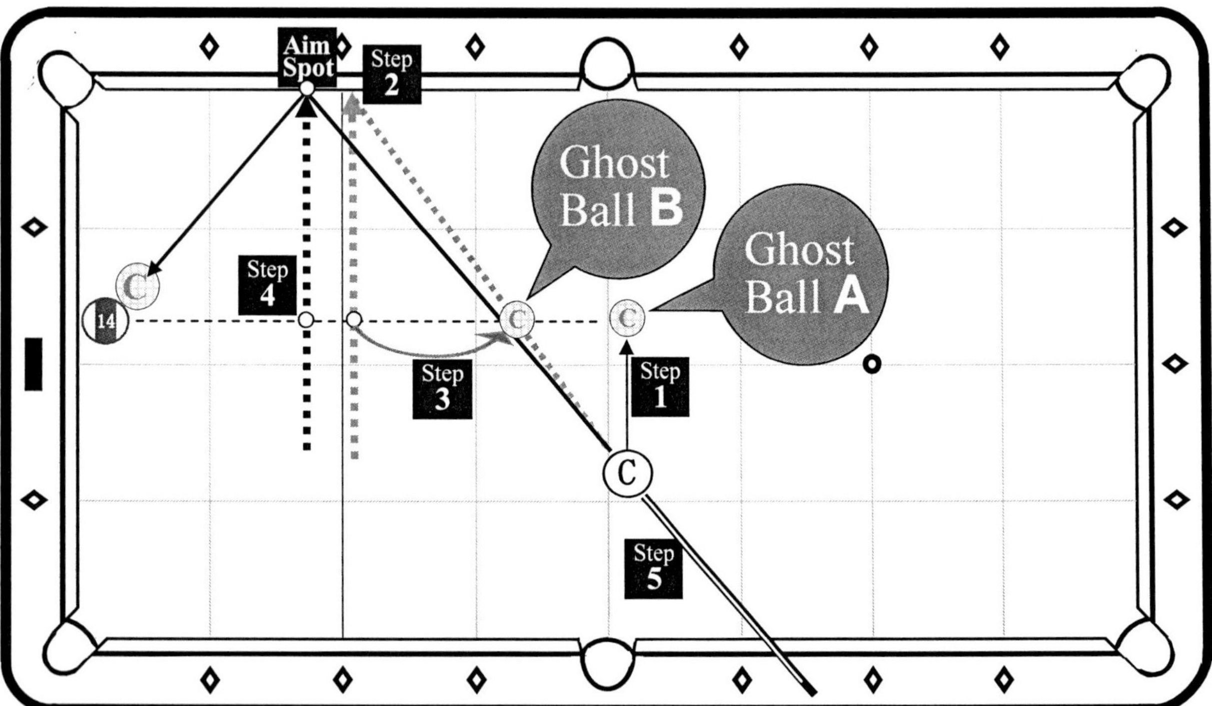

Foot Notes

In no time you'll see the ghost balls, the perpendicular line and the point on the rail to aim at in less than 10 seconds.

This is the most accurate system for open table one rail kicks.

If you're still not clear how It's done, <u>you may need to watch it on the DVD.</u>

Advanced Option

1. Extend your arm enough so you're looking through the Tip of your index finger to see each of the table and rail positions.
2. Position your body squarely in front of each of the gray and black dashed lines.
3. In the Step 5 position, stand behind the cue and pull the cue butt directly to yourself. Keep the Tip on the aiming path.

PROBLEM: 1. How to find the AIM SPOT on the rail.
2. Cue ball is **BELOW** the object ball.

BASIC:

Step 1. PUSH UP the Tip of the cue, from the cue ball, until it is perpendicular to the 14 ball (see Ghost Ball A above).

Step 2. Use your extended left index finger to find the midway point between Ghost Ball A and the 14 ball. Visually slide the Tip of your finger to the rail, then place the cue Tip to the rail (the gray dash line follows these moves).

Step 3. Pivot the butt back over the cue ball. Draw the tip of the shaft back again, stopping the Tip on the perpendicular line (See the Ghost Ball B position with the gray dotted line above for making this move).

Step 4. Like **Step 2,** use your finger and find the midway point between Ghost Ball B and the 14 ball, then follow the black dashed line up to the rail. **That's the exact spot you aim at when you are ready to shoot.**

Step 5. Aim and shoot at the **AIM SPOT** on the rail using a 3 to 5 speed, with ½ Tip above center English.

ADVANCED: This technique takes less than 7 seconds when you use your cue and your free hand together to determine the aiming spot.

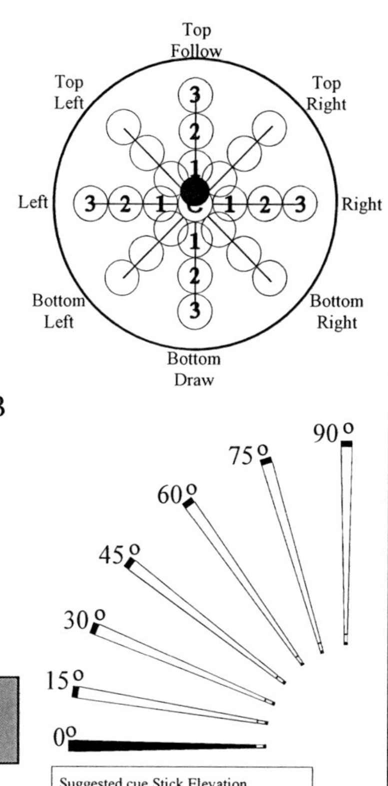

1 RAIL KICK - CUE BALL LOW

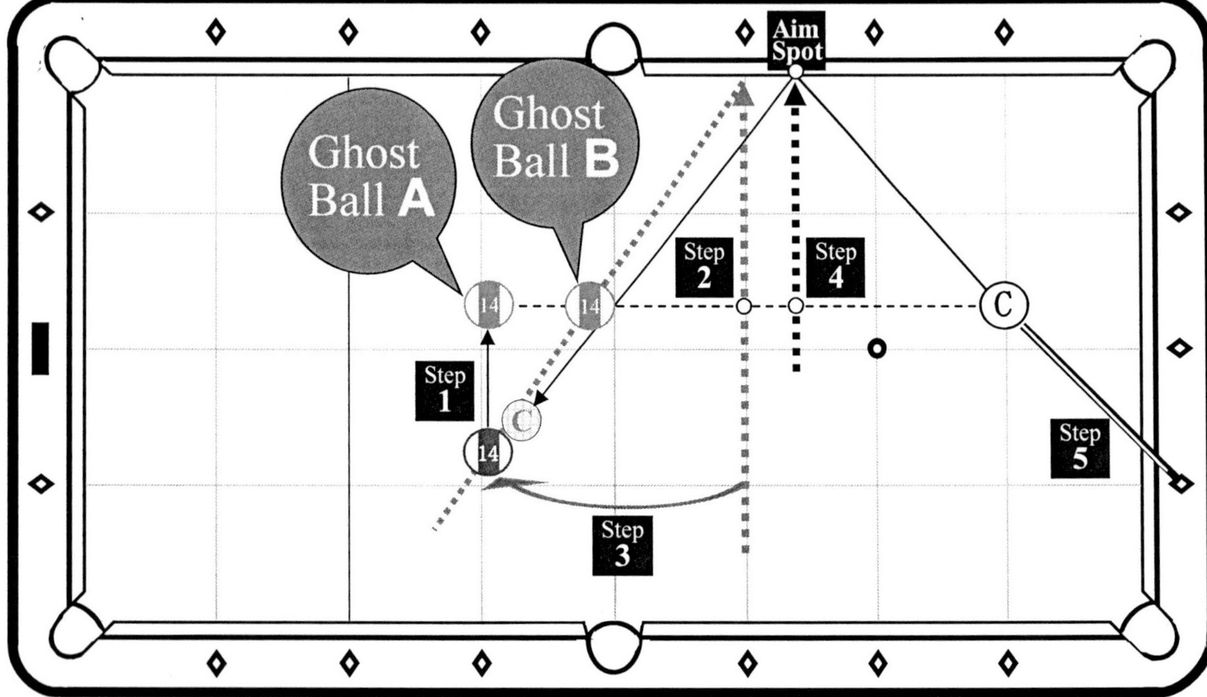

Foot Notes

In no time you'll see the ghost balls, the perpendicular line and the point on the rail to aim at in less than 10 seconds.

This is the most accurate system for open table one rail kicks.

If you're still not clear how It's done, you may need to watch it on the DVD.

Advanced Option

1. Extend your arm enough so you're looking through the Tip of your index finger to see each of the table and rail positions.
2. Position your body squarely in front of each of the gray and black dashed lines.
3. In the Step 5 position, stand behind the cue and pull the cue butt directly to yourself. Keep the Tip on the aiming path.

PROBLEM: 1. How to find the AIM SPOT on the rail.
2. Cue ball is **ABOVE** the object ball.

BASIC:

Step 1. PUSH UP the Tip of the cue, from the object ball, until it is perpendicular to the cue ball (see Ghost Ball A above).

Step 2. Use your extended left index finger to find the midway point between Ghost Ball A and the cue ball. Visually slide the Tip of your finger to the rail, then place the cue Tip to the rail (the gray dash line follows these moves).

Step 3. Pivot the butt back over the cue ball. Draw the tip of the shaft back again, stopping the Tip on the perpendicular line (See the Ghost Ball B position with the gray dotted line above for making this move).

Step 4. Like **Step 2,** use your finger and find the midway point between Ghost Ball B and the cue ball, then follow the black dashed line up to the rail. **That's the exact spot you aim at when you are ready to shoot.**

Step 5. Aim and shoot at the **AIM SPOT** on the rail using a 3 to 5 speed, with ½ Tip above center English.

ADVANCED: This is the reverse of shot **#9** and also takes less than 7 seconds to determine the aiming spot.

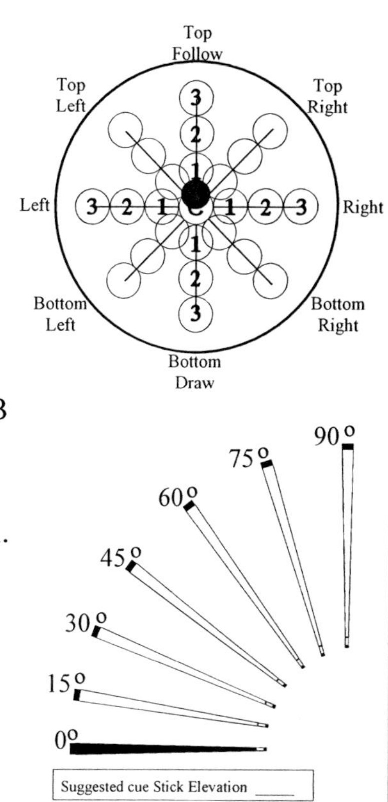

12 1 RAIL KICK - CUE BALL HIGH

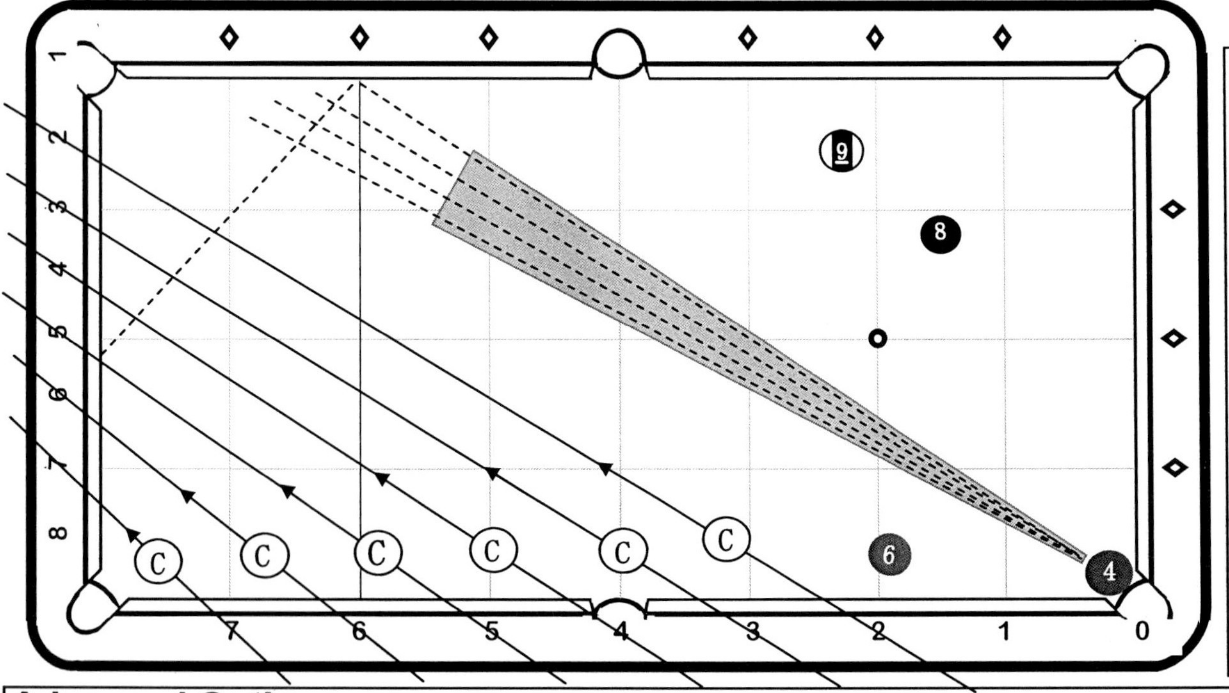

Foot Notes

The lower the side rail number, the longer the cue ball path. You may need to adjust the Running English to the cue ball.

As the side rail numbers get higher, use less Running English on the cue ball. Enjoy discovering what works for you.

Advanced Option

An Advanced Option shot does not always mean that that's the better way to make this shot.

PROBLEM: 1. Cue ball is blocked for a straight in shot.
2. Other object balls are blocking a simple one rail kick shot.

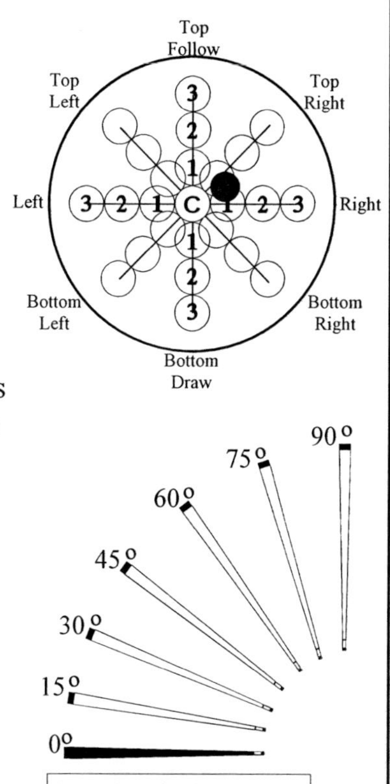

BASIC:

1. Start from the 4 ball in the corner pocket, count that pocket as 0, (zero) and each Diamond moving up the long rail, count a full number value (see the Diamond 0 to 7 count on the tables long rail above).

NOTE: This shot can be done form either side or direction on the table.

2. Diagonally, on the other end of the table, start counting the corner pocket as number 1. Each half Diamond space receives one full number value (see the 1 through 8 on the short rail above).
3. Connect the matching numbers for the two rails.
4. Use a 4 to 5 Speed Stroke keeping your cue stick level through the shot.
5. Starting from Diamond #2, apply Running English.
6. Adjust from Running English to Soft English as you move up the long rail toward the number 7 Diamond. Test this shot during warm up to be sure you know how the rails and your Running English are responding.

 SAME SIDE RAIL KICK 1

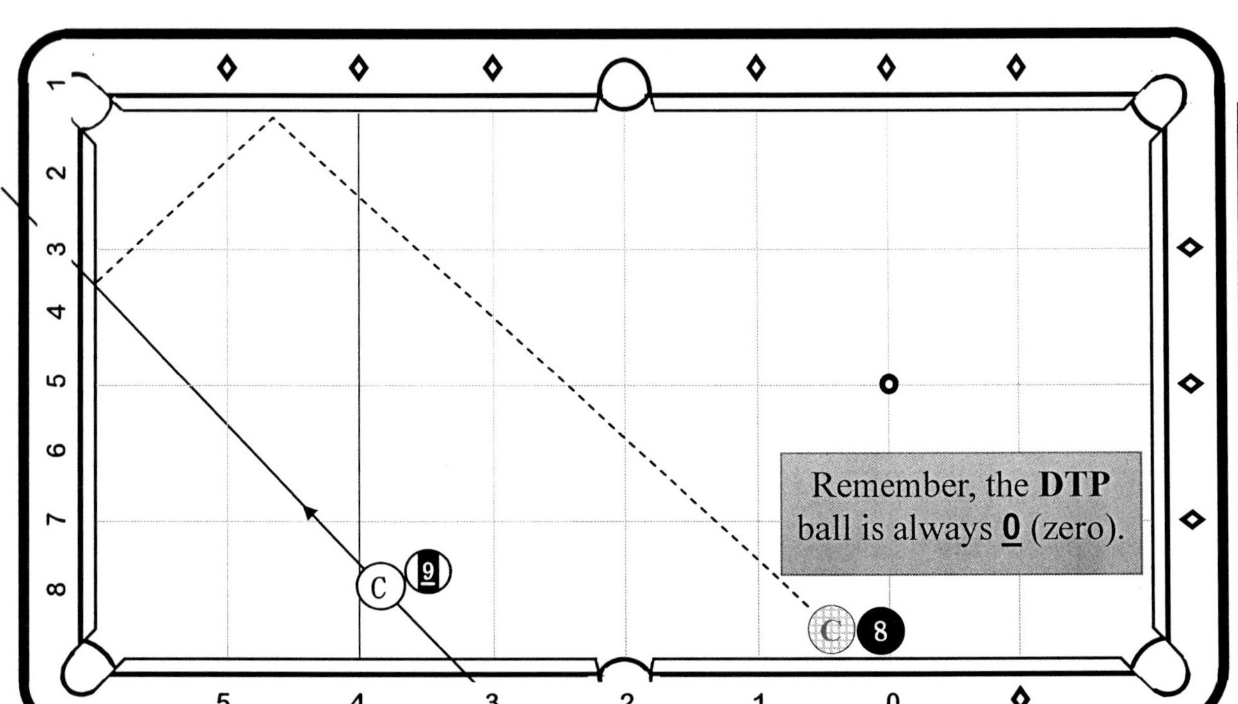

Foot Notes

The lower the side rail number, the longer the cue ball path. Adjust from Running English to Soft English as you move up the rail.

As the side rail numbers get higher, use less Running English on the cue ball. Enjoy discovering what works for you.

Advanced Option

The more you practice these shot situations, the more accurate you're going to become at determining the English to use. Don't wait for a game situation to come up to try to remember how much English to apply.

PROBLEM: 1. Cue ball is blocked for a straight-in shot on the 8 ball.
2. 9 ball and cue ball are frozen blocking a kick shot to the opposite side rail.

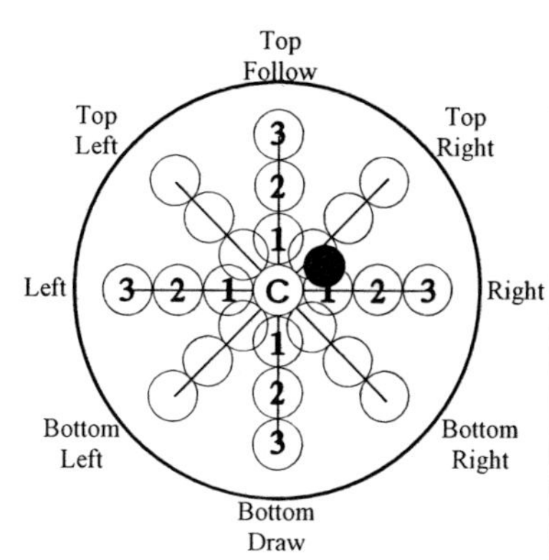

BASIC:

1. Starting from the 8 ball on the rail, that Diamond location is 0. **Remember, wherever the target object ball (DTP) is, that location is always counted as 0.** From that point start moving left to apply a number value for each Diamond until you reach the cue ball (see Diamond count 0 to 5 above).

NOTE: Everything works in reverse if you're on the other side of the table.

2. Diagonally, on the other end of the table, start counting from the corner pocket as number 1. Each half Diamond space receives one full number value (see the 1 to 8 on the short rail above).
3. Connect the matching numbers for the two rails until you can find (3 to 3).
4. Use a 4 to 5 speed stroke and keep your cue stick level.
5. Use Running English when the cue ball is close to the object ball and gradually move closer to Soft English as the cue ball moves away from the object ball.

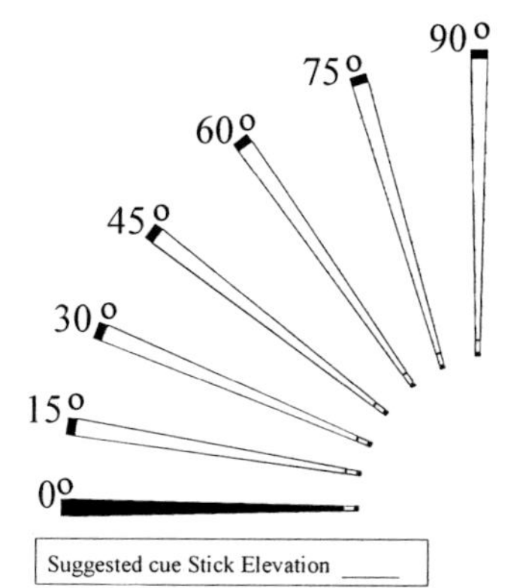

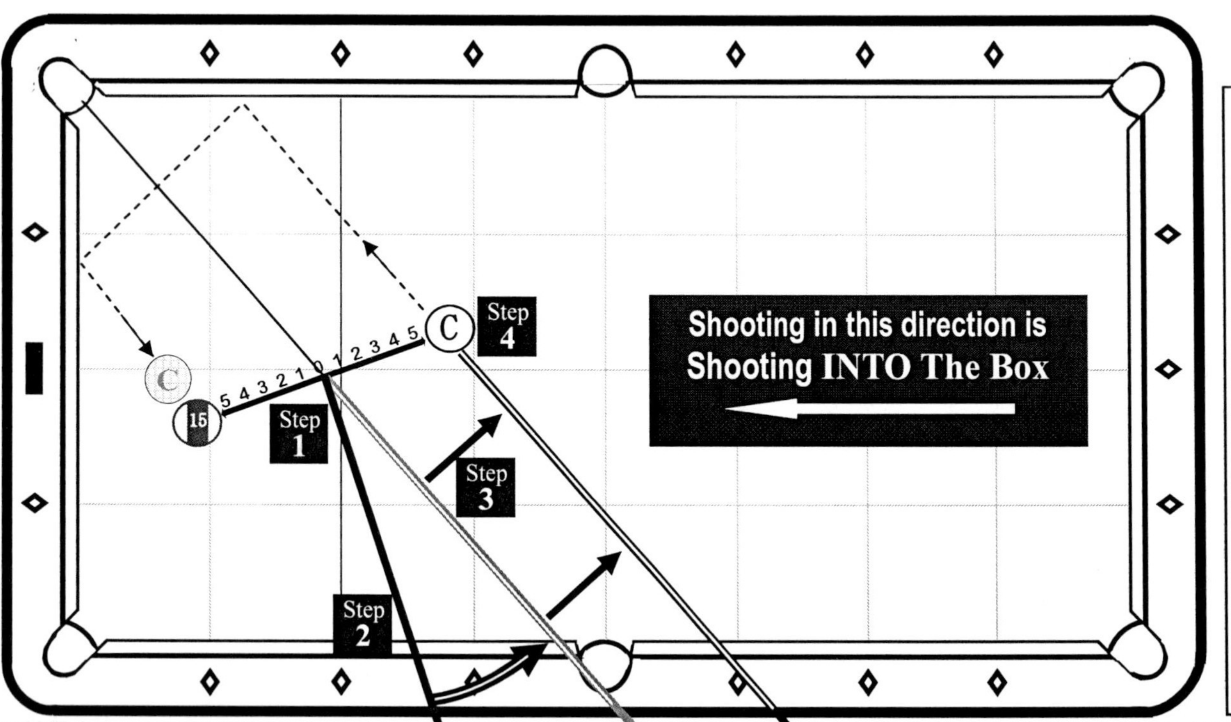

Foot Notes

Whenever you shoot toward the object ball (see direction arrow of shot), this is called, "Shooting Into The Box" and always uses Running English. Speed and cushion quality may require adjusting cue ball English.

Advanced Option

Even if the cue ball were in the other half of the table (on the right side as you see it), this would still be considered as shooting into the box because the initial direction of the cue ball is shot toward the direction of the box (the half table) the object ball is in.

PROBLEM: 1. Cue ball is blocked for a straight or one rail kick shot.

BASIC:

Step 1. Place the Tip of your cue stick on the table at the mid point between the cue ball and the target object ball. Stand squarely facing between the two balls lined up, making a perfect 90° T-square (see the bold black lines above).

Step 2. Let the Tip of your cue continue to rest on the table and pivot the butt until the entire cue stick points directly into the corner pocket that the cue ball will pass in front of after it hits the first rail (the diagram above shows the cue pivots with the black arrow line swinging to the right and becoming the gray line).

Step 3. Shift the cue stick perfectly parallel until it points directly at the cue ball. Be sure the shaft and butt ends move evenly. Misjudging the parallel shifting move, over or under, as little as one inch, can result in missing the object ball.

Step 4. Use Running English when you're shooting **INTO** the box ("The Box" means one half side of the pool table, because it's square in shape).

Step 5. Shoot with a level cue stick, smooth follow-through and release the shot with a 3 to 5 speed stroke.

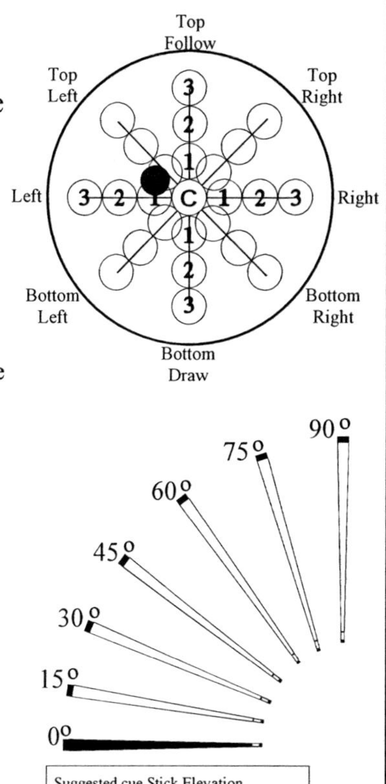

 2 RAIL KICK - INTO THE BOX

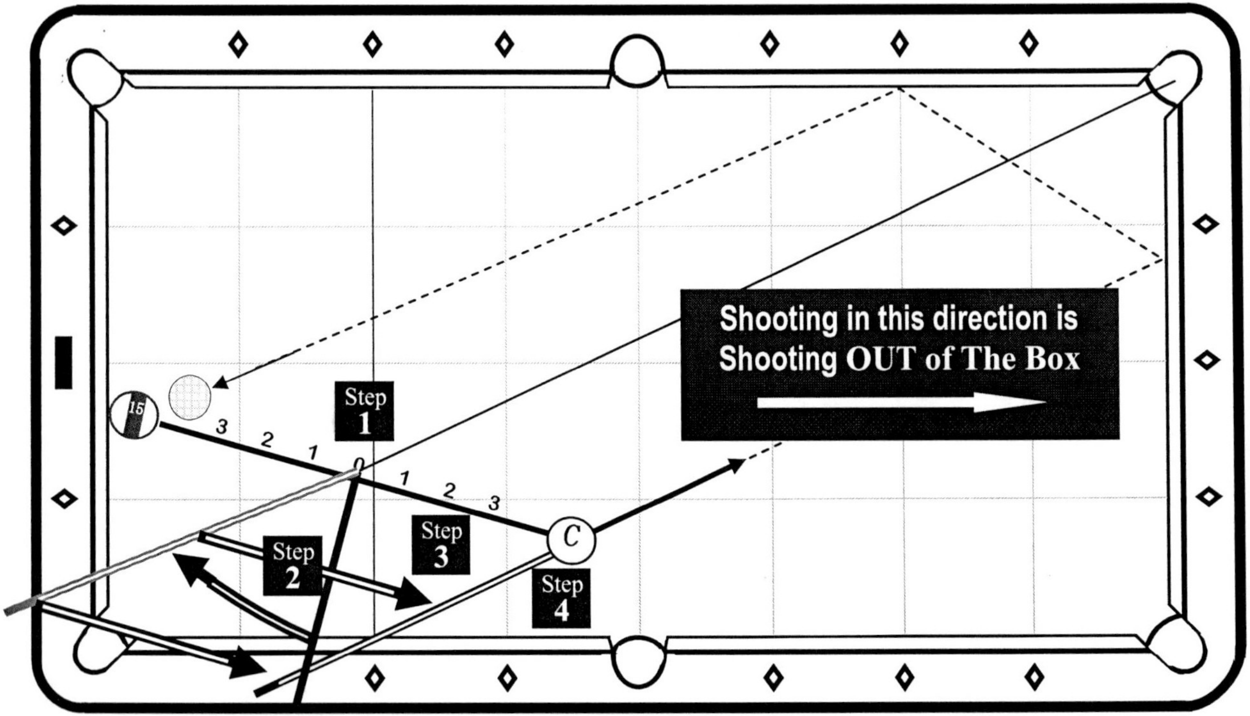

Shooting in this direction is Shooting **OUT of The Box**

Step 1

Step 2

Step 3

Step 4

Foot Notes

When shooting ***Out Of The Box****, away from the object ball (to the other half of the table, then back into the original half of the table) use* ***Soft English: 1 Tip above the center then ⅛ to ¼ Tip*** *to the side (always on the side you want the cue ball to SPIN off of the first rail that's contacted).*

Advanced Option

Even if the cue ball were in the other half of the table (on the right side as you see it), this would still be considered as shooting Out of the box because the initial direction of the cue ball is shot away from the direction of the box the object ball is in.

PROBLEM: 1. The cue ball is blocked for a straight or one rail kick shot.

BASIC:

Step 1. Place the Tip of your cue stick on the table at the mid point between the cue ball and the target object ball. Stand squarely facing between the two balls lined up, making a perfect 90° T-square (see the bold black lines above).

Step 2. Let the Tip of your cue continue to rest on the table and pivot the butt until the entire cue stick points directly into the corner pocket that the cue ball will pass in front of after it hits the first rail (the diagram above shows the cue pivots with the black arrow line swinging to the right and becoming the gray line).

Step 3. Shift the cue stick perfectly parallel until it points directly at the cue ball. Be sure the shaft and butt ends move evenly. Misjudging the parallel shifting move, over or under, as little as one inch, can result in missing the object ball.

Step 4. Use Running English when you're shooting **INTO** the box ("The Box" means one half side of the pool table, because it's square in shape).

Step 5. Shoot with a level cue stick, smooth follow-through and release the shot with a 3 to 5 speed stroke.

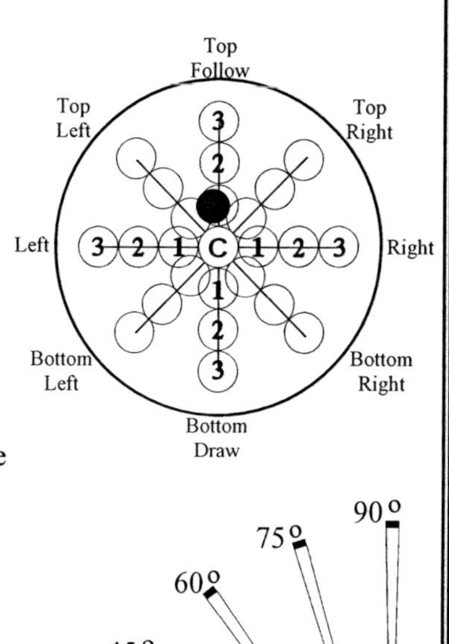

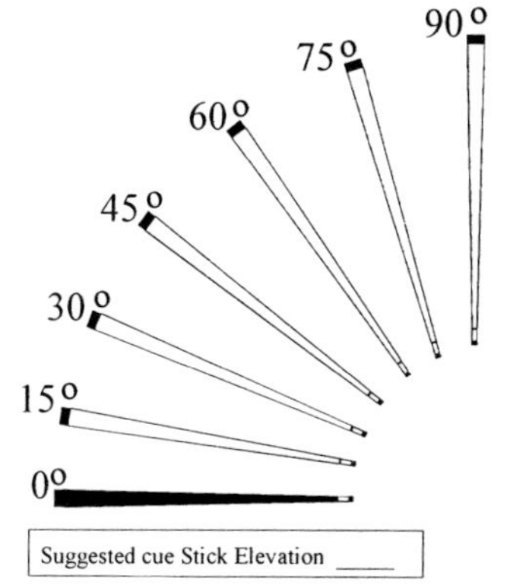

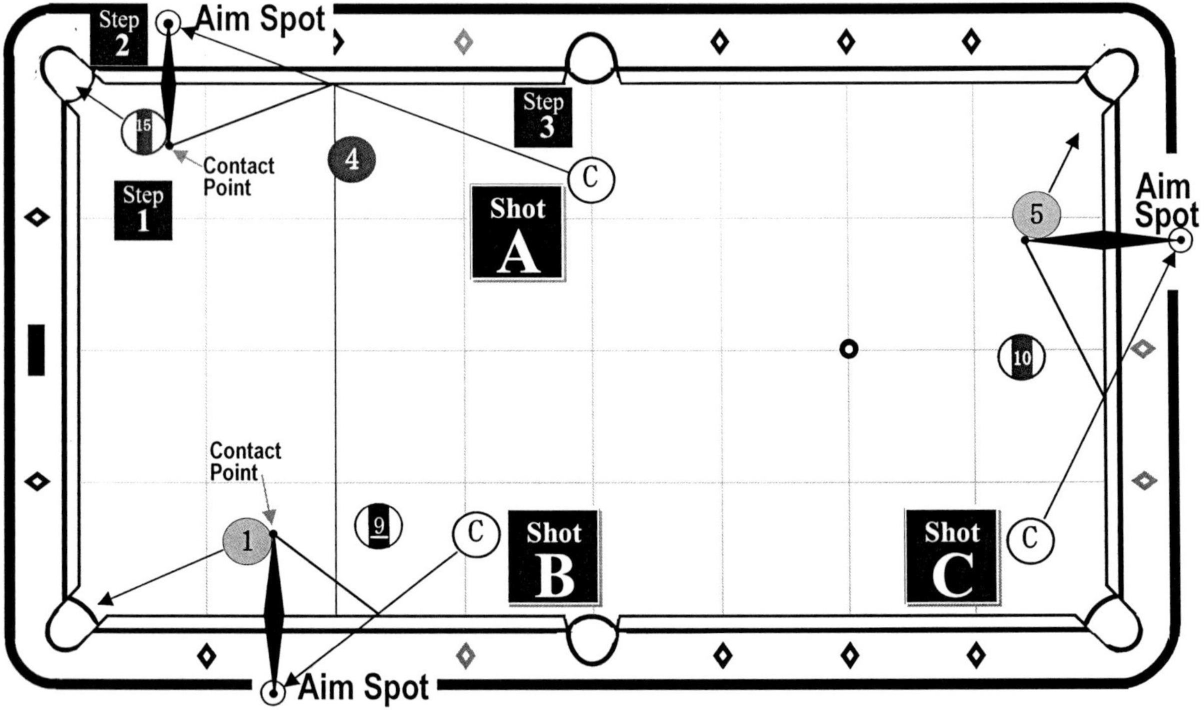

Step 2

Aim Spot

Step 3

15

Contact Point

4

C

Step 1

Shot A

5

Aim Spot

10

Contact Point

1

9

C

Shot B

Shot C

C

Aim Spot

Foot Notes

Keep your eye on the ***Aim Spot*** *on the rail while you walk around the table to set up for the shot.*

When you get back behind the cue ball, extend your cue out and touch the ***Aim Spot*** *with the Tip of your cue.*

Look down from the shaft and take notice to where the cue ball will touch.

Advanced Option

If the **Contact Point** to the rail is 5½ inches, the extended line to the **Aim Spot** should be 5½ inches; a mirror image.

PROBLEM: 1. Cue ball is blocked for a straight shot on the object ball.

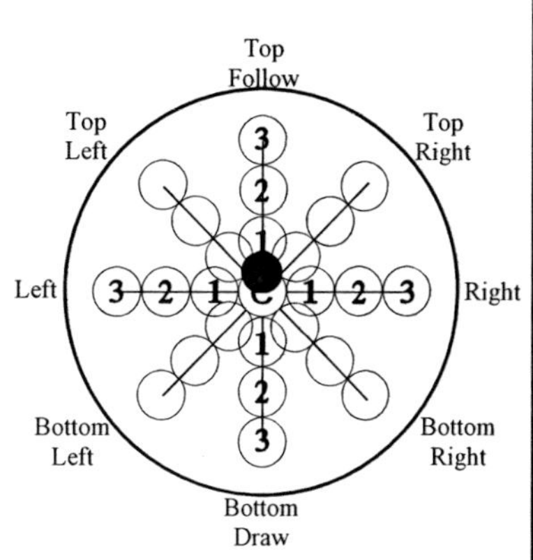

BASIC:

Step 1. Determine the contact point on the object ball you want to hit.

Step 2. Use your shaft or finger to measure the perpendicular distance from the contact point (from **Step 1**) to the contact edge of rail.

From the contact edge of the rail (see the Diamond shaped line on the rail), measure an equal distance that extends over the rail (like an exact mirror image from the table side). That is how to determine the Aim Spot.

Step 3. Shoot directly at the Aim Spot. The cue ball will contact the rail at the exact spot needed to bank off and hit the contact point on the object ball that was selected in **Step 1** above.

1. Center ball or ½ Tip above the center of the cue ball.
2. Keep the cue stick level.
3. Use a 2 or 3 Speed Stroke.
4. Apply a smooth follow through

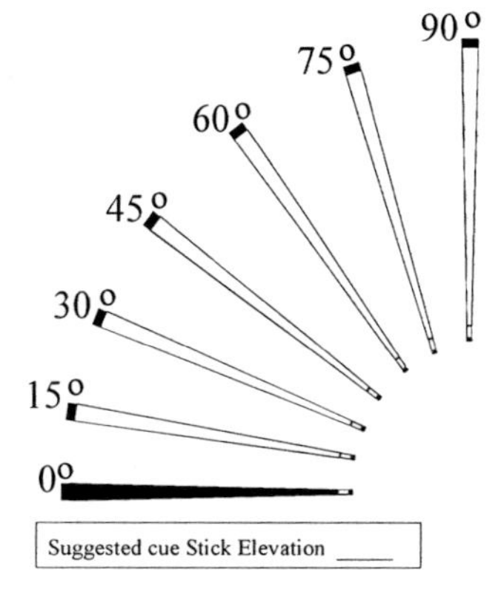

17 RAIL FIRST KICK SHOT 1

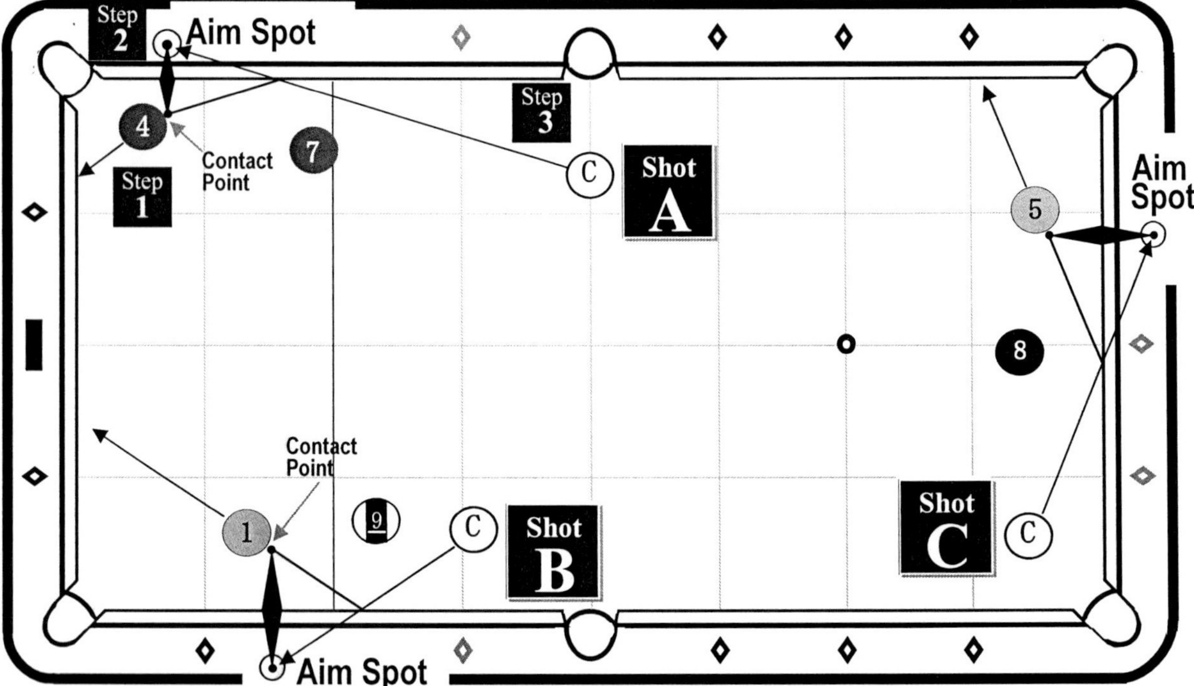

Foot Notes

*Keep your eye on the **Aim Spot** on the rail while you walk around the table to set up for the shot.*

*When you get back behind the cue ball, extend your cue out and touch the **Aim Spot** with the Tip of your cue.*

Look down from the shaft and take notice to where the cue ball will touch.

Advanced Option

When the blocking ball is cutting off the natural angle cue ball roll, keep the same Aim Spot and:

1. Add Top English to lengthen the angle the cue ball comes off the rail, causing a fatter hit.
2. Add Draw to shorten the cue ball angle off the rail, causing a thinner hit on the Aim Spot.

PROBLEM: 1. Cue ball is blocked for a straight shot on the object ball.

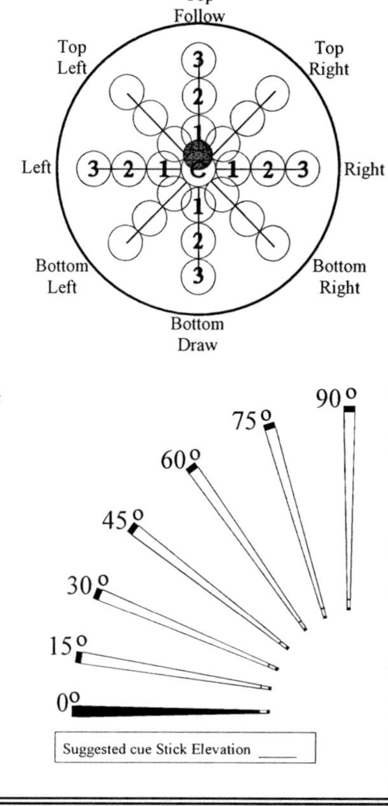

BASIC:

Step 1. Determine the contact point on the object ball you want to hit.

Step 2. Use your shaft or finger to measure the perpendicular distance from the contact point (from **Step 1**) to the contact edge of rail.

From the contact edge of the rail (see the Diamond shaped line on the rail), measure an equal distance that extends over the rail (like an exact mirror image from the table side). That is how to determine the Aim Spot.

Step 3. Shoot directly at the Aim Spot. The cue ball will contact the rail at the exact spot needed to bank off and hit the contact point on the object ball that was selected from **Step 1** above.

1. Center ball or ½ Tip above the center of the cue ball.
2. Keep the cue stick level.
3. Use a 2 or 3 Speed Stroke.
4. Apply a smooth follow through

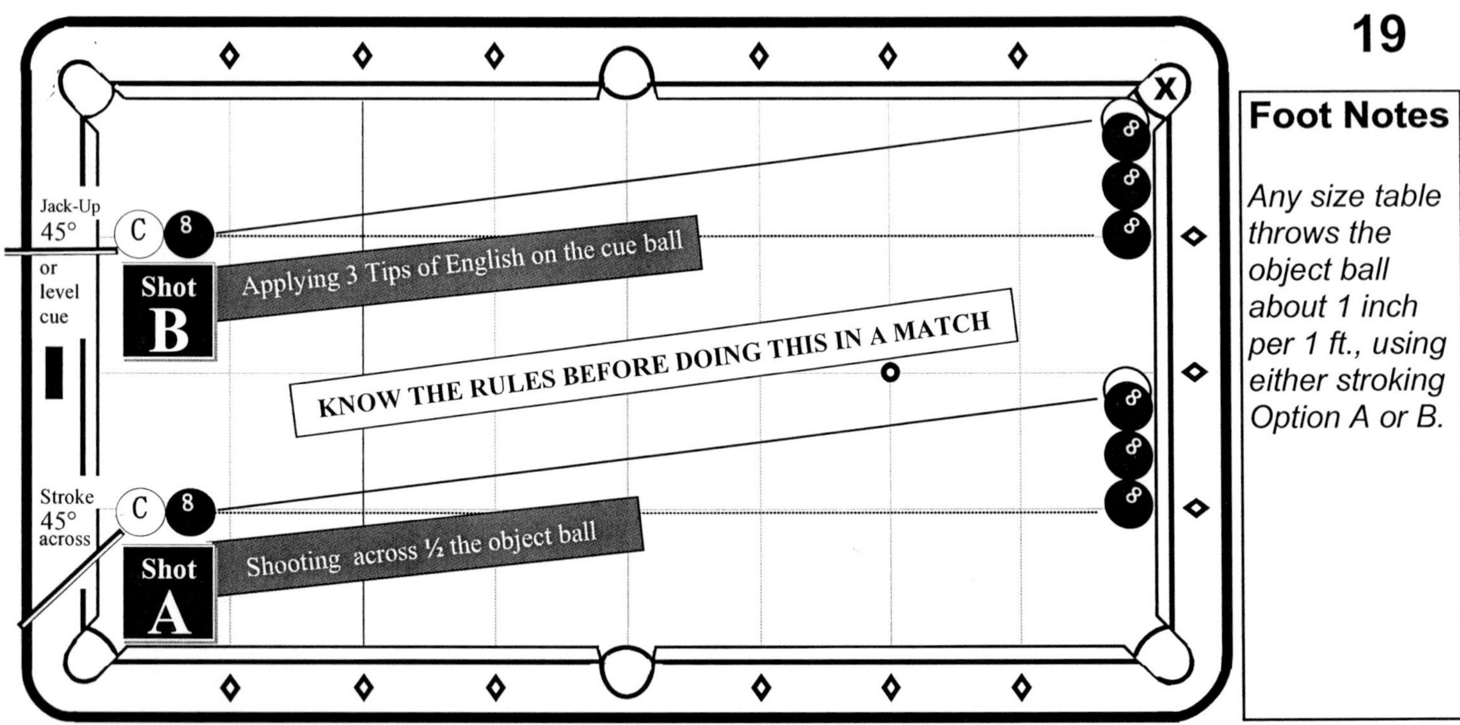

Foot Notes

Any size table throws the object ball about 1 inch per 1 ft., using either stroking Option A or B.

Advanced Option

The illustration above is based on a 9 foot table, with the cue ball and 8 ball frozen together: On a 9' table, the frozen balls would be about 96 inches away from the other end of the table, about 8½ feet away, which equals about 9 inches of throw.

PROBLEM: 1. Cue ball and object ball are frozen together.

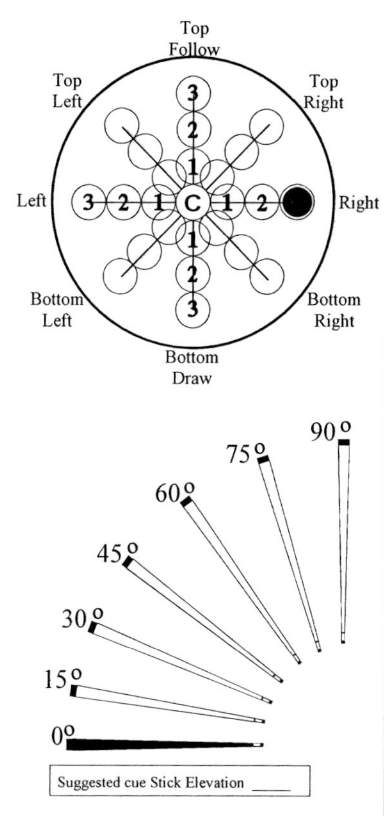

BASIC:

When two pool balls are touching, it is said that they are frozen. When two balls are frozen, it is said that the balls can be thrown. Throwing a frozen pool ball is accomplished by one of two ways.

1. First, aim the cue stick so as to shoot about 45° across the line of the two frozen balls **(see Option A).**
2. The second way to throw a frozen ball is to apply SPIN or English on the opposite side of the cue ball from the direction you want the object ball to go **(see Option B)**.

Note: Either Option works. What matters is to know the rules before shooting. Ask an official or your opponent before you shoot to avoid a foul or needless delay by a game distraction.

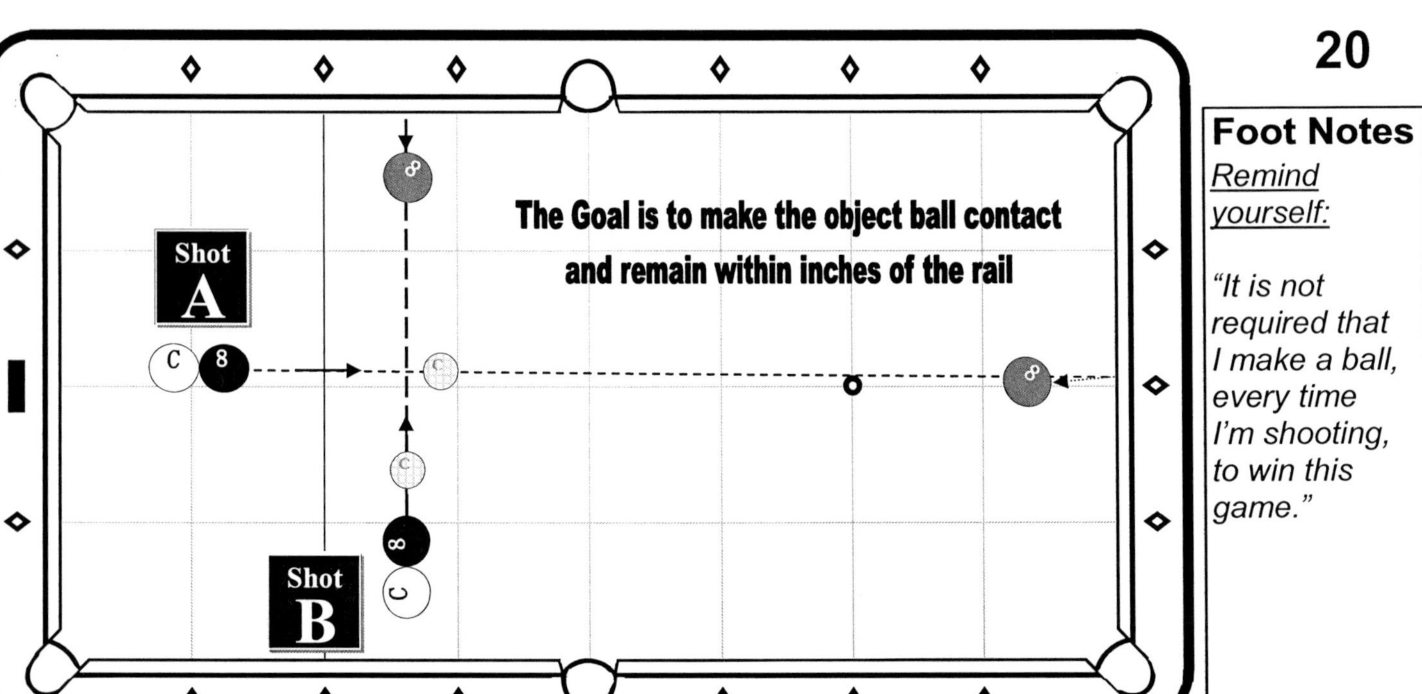

Foot Notes

Remind yourself:

"It is not required that I make a ball, every time I'm shooting, to win this game."

Advanced Option

Cue ball and object ball are frozen and NOT facing toward a corner pocket.
This is your first sign to get defensive, not disgusted.

PROBLEM: 1. Cue ball and object ball are frozen together.

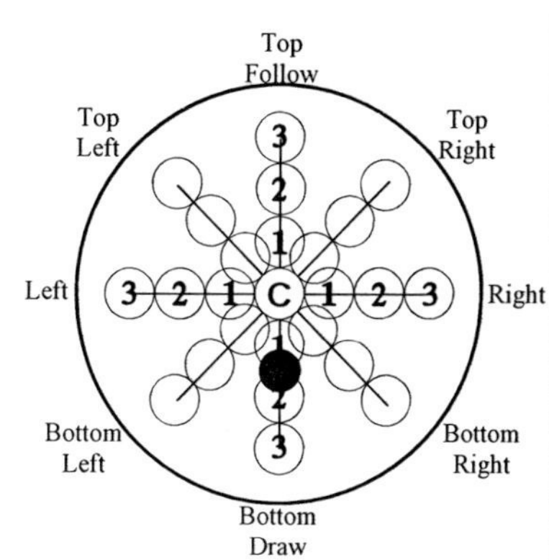

BASIC:

Shot A:
1. 30° elevated cue.
2. 1 Tip below center English.
3. 2 Speed Stroke.

Shot B:
1. 30° elevated cue.
2. 1 Tip below center English.
3. 1 Speed Stroke.

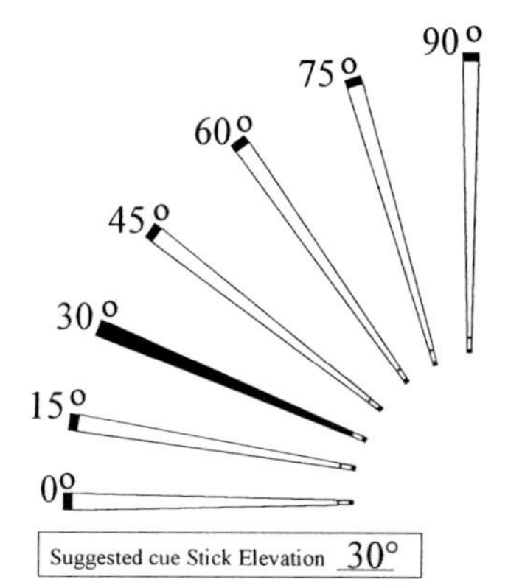

NOTE: BE SURE THE 8 BALL HITS THE RAIL SO YOU DON'T CAUSE A TABLE SCRATCH AND GIVE UP BALL IN HAND.

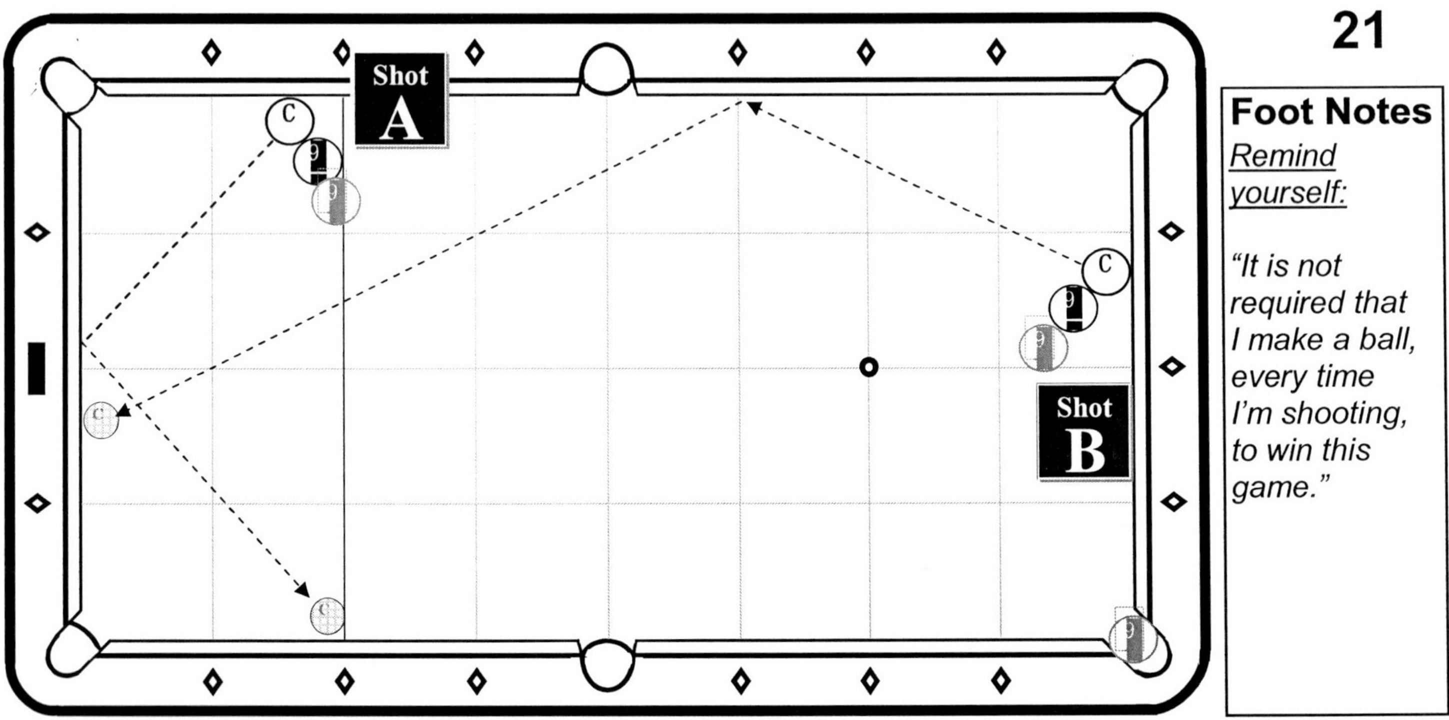

Foot Notes

<u>*Remind yourself:*</u>

"It is not required that I make a ball, every time I'm shooting, to win this game."

Advanced Option

Here is a helpful Tip that really works. Walk to the side of the table where you want the cue ball to come to a stop. Place your finger or hand on that spot where you want the cue ball to land. Hold it there for about 3 seconds and say to yourself, *"I intend to make the cue ball land right on this spot."* You will make the cue ball land on that exact spot. Really!

PROBLEM: 1. Cue ball and object ball are frozen together.

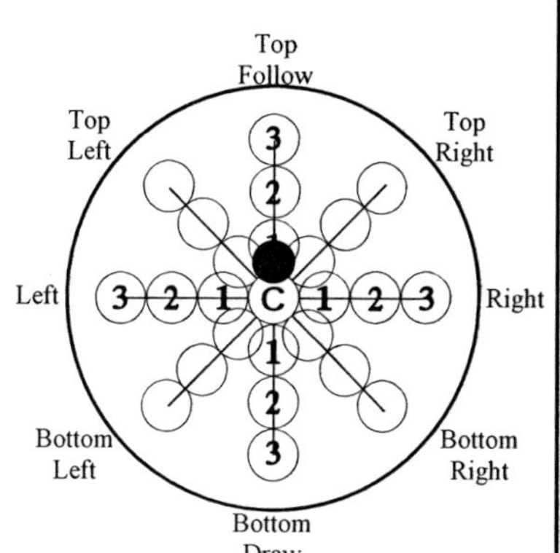

BASIC:

1. Shoot with a level cue and a smooth, rhythmic stroke.

2. Being on the rail, you will automatically hit the cue ball with top English, however, don't over-hit the ball so as to cause an over SPIN.

3. Be sure to shoot through the 9 ball ever so thin so as to make the object ball move as little as possible.

4. Your main focus is on the cue ball speed; making the cue ball land exactly where you want it to land. Remember, it must touch a rail after it has grazed off the object ball.

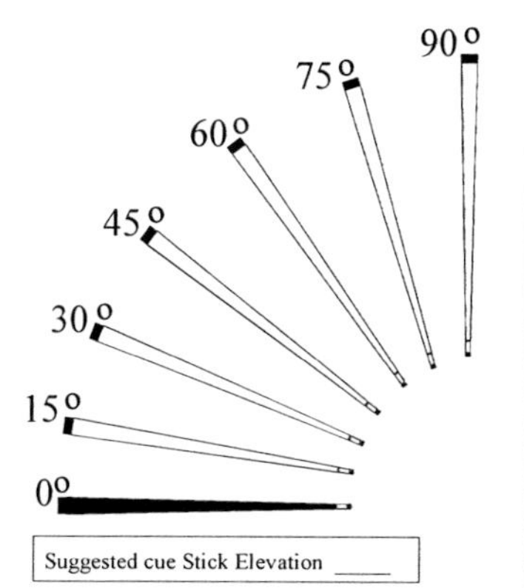

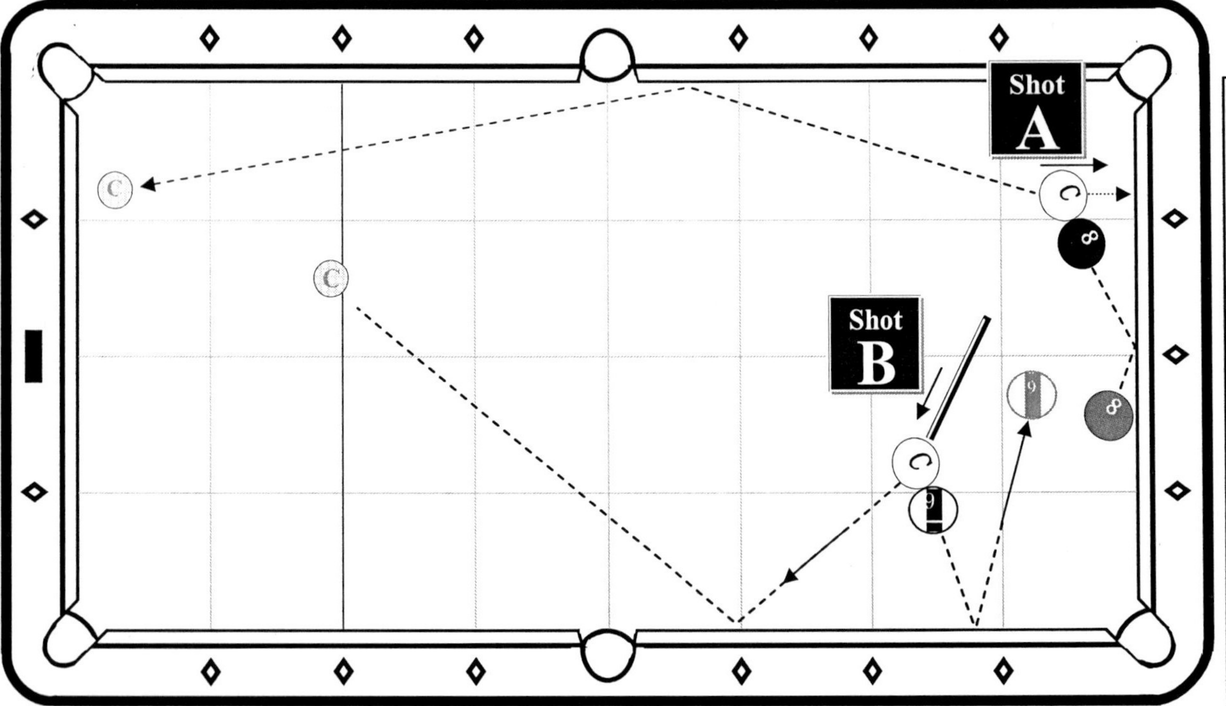

Foot Notes

Remind yourself:

"It is not required that I make a ball, every time I'm shooting, to win this game."

Advanced Option

Remember, when you face the tough shots, that is your first sign to get defensive, not disgusted.

PROBLEM: 1. Cue ball and object ball are frozen together.

BASIC:

Shots A or B are both shot with a 30° elevated cue.

1. Use 1 Tip below center English.

2. Use a 3 to 4 Speed Stroke .

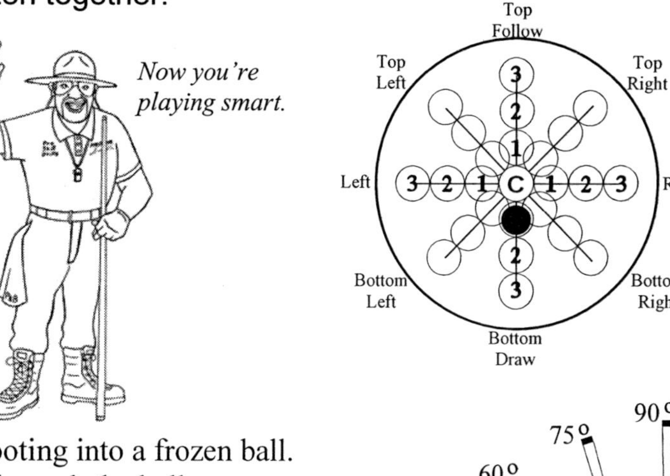

NOTE: Double check to be sure of the rules on shooting into a frozen ball.

- Some allow you to shoot with a level cue straight through the ball.
- Some require you to be jacked up 45°.
- Some say you can use a level cue but you must shoot at least 45° across the ball.

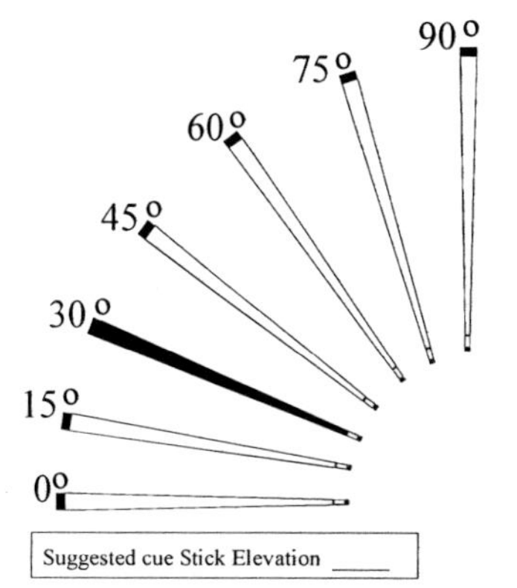

22 FROZEN SHOTS 4

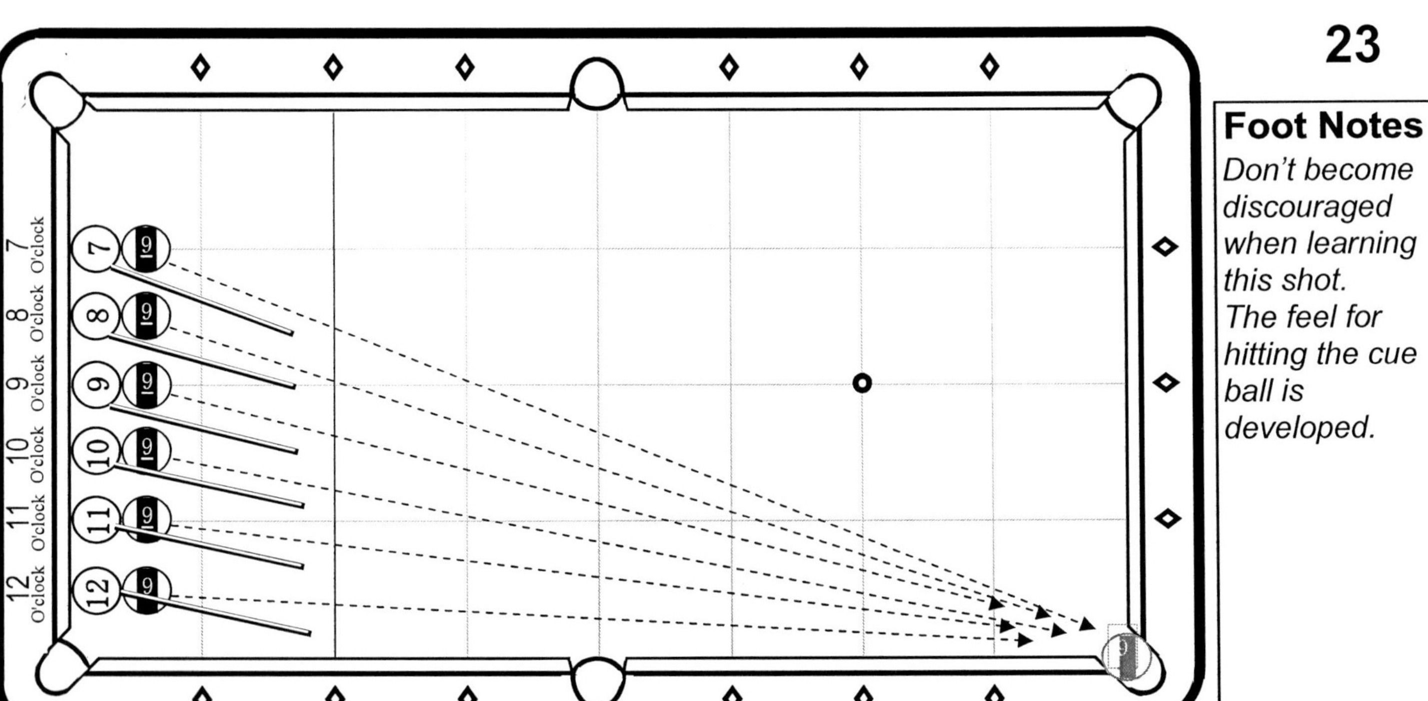

Foot Notes

Don't become discouraged when learning this shot.
The feel for hitting the cue ball is developed.

Advanced Option

This may not work so well on some bar box tables.
From the Pool Players 10 Commandments #4: <u>Know Thy Rails</u>!

PROBLEM: 1. Cue ball and object ball are frozen together.

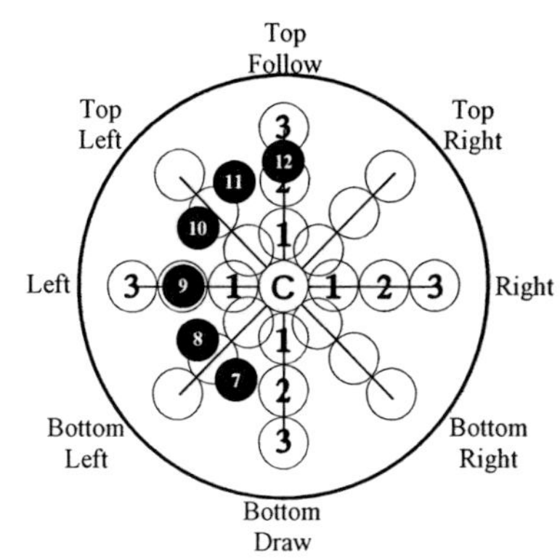

BASIC:

This shot is unique because it's shot in reverse. You shoot into the rail and the cue ball snaps out, catching the object ball at the right angle to cut it into the corner pocket.

(see the dash lines above tracking toward the corner pocket)

1. 2 Tips from center in the O'clock positions from 12 to 7.
2. A level to maximum 15° raised cue stick.
3. A high, towering raised closed hand bridge.
4. Stroke through the top of the cue ball with the power of a 4 to 5 Speed Stroke. The rail adds more speed to the object ball automatically.

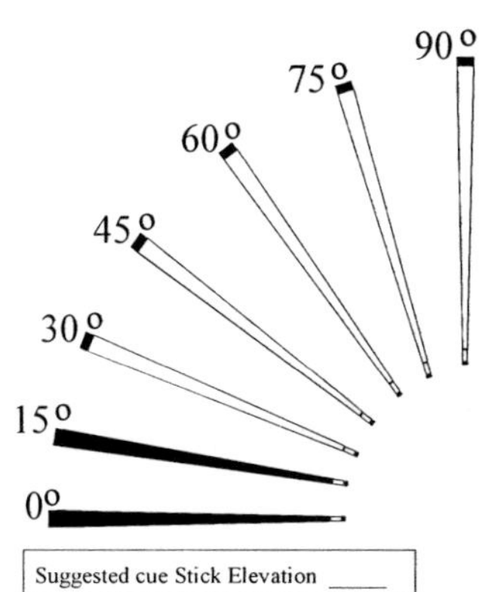

The matching numbers on each of the cue balls above on the short rail and the Striking Points on the cue ball indicate the contact spot to hit on the cue ball.

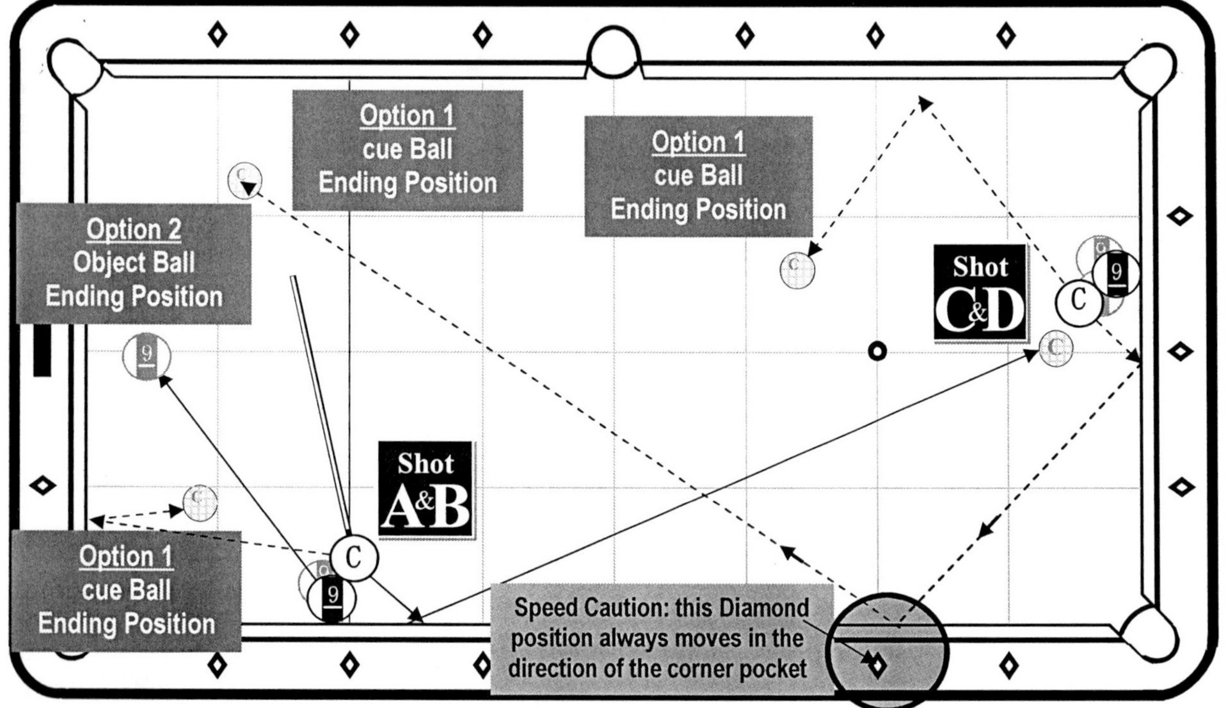

Foot Notes

For the other 3 Shot Options:

You won't need to call for someone to watch the hit. Trust me on this one; everyone will see if the object ball flinches or not. Your job is to make sure it "only flinches" and that the cue ball is out of there.

Advanced Option

This shot also works when the balls are NOT frozen but are very close.

PROBLEM: 1. Cue ball and object ball are frozen together.

BASIC:

Notice in Shot A&B, you can play it two different ways. However, Option 2 is the most critical of the two. You must focus on the speed of the object ball so it comes off the rail and rolls out to the middle of the table, as close to the short rail as possible. You don't want to under or over hit and leave it in front of a corner pocket. Play it this way:

1. Shoot with a 30° elevated cue.
2. 1 Tip below center.
3. Aim ⅛" or thinner into the object ball.
4. Use a short but smooth snapping stroke. This stroke will prevent a double hit.

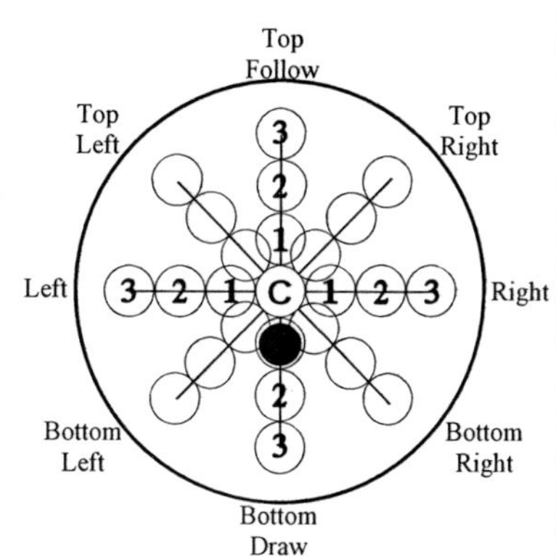

Shot C&D, also have two options. Take time to test each way to get the feel for how each option plays out. Remember, only focus on the speed of one of the balls in the shot. Don't ever try to control both ball speeds during the shot.

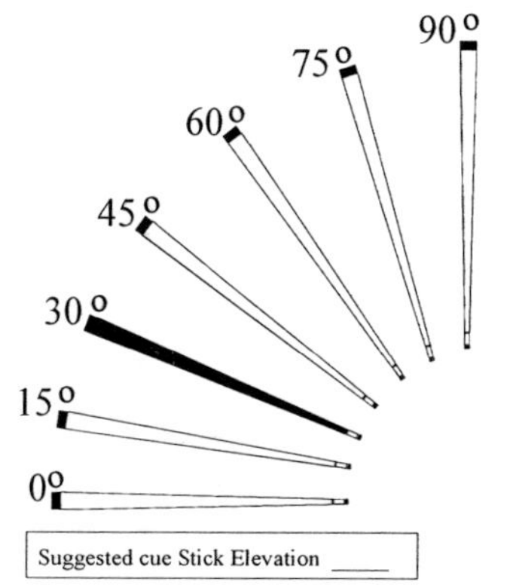

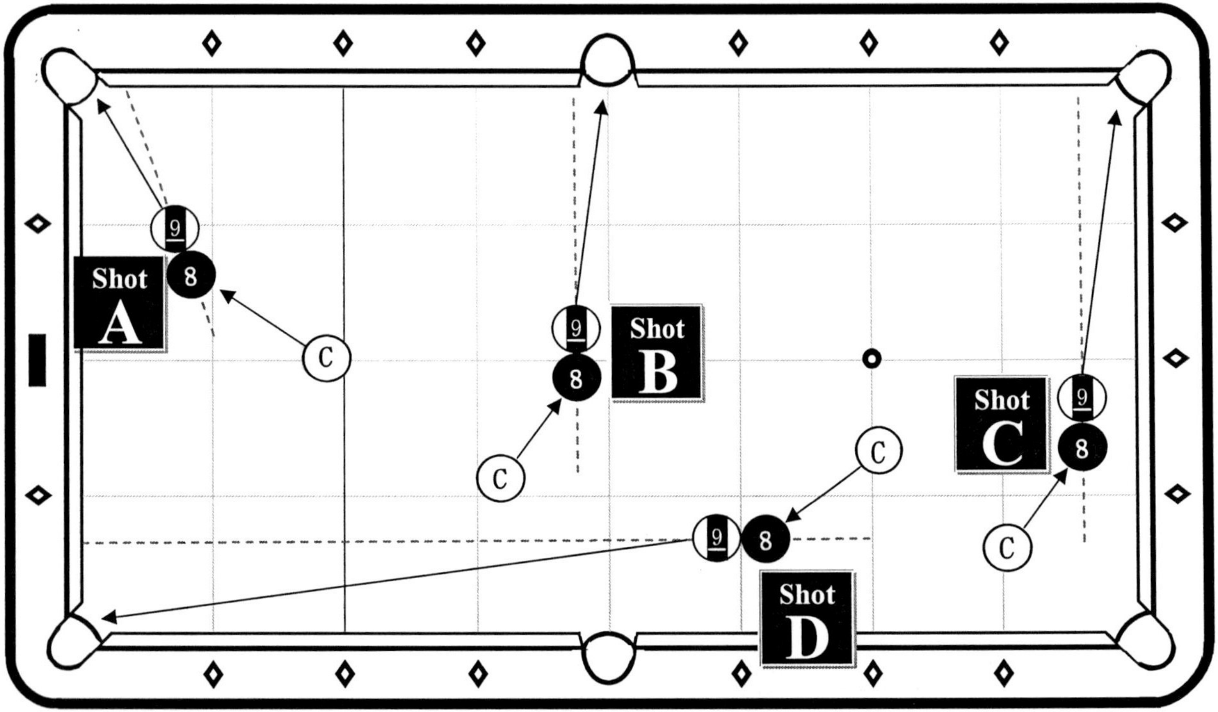

Shot A

Shot B

Shot C

Shot D

Foot Notes

1, 2, or 3 Tips of Inside English will affect the amount of reverse rotation on the first ball hit.

Advanced Option

1. Hitting the first object ball with a ½ ball hit will cause the second ball to throw 1 inch for every 1 foot (Diamond) it travels.
2. If you have less angle into the first object ball but can add English, this can increase the throw as well.
3. Balls that are dirty or freshly polished will be further impacted by adding 1 Tip of Top or Draw English.

PROBLEM: 1. Two other object balls are frozen but not directly facing into a pocket.

BASIC:

This is also called a THROW SHOT. You actually change the direction the balls are pointing toward, causing the last ball to roll in a different direction.

This is different from the cue ball being frozen to the object ball (see #19). Here two object balls are frozen together and the cue ball is hitting the first object ball from an angle. Note that adding additional cue ball English can cause some additional redirection of the second object ball.

WARNING: SHOOTING DIRECTLY INTO TWO FROZEN BALLS, IN A STRAIGHT LINE, WITH ANY AMOUNT OF CUE BALL SPIN, WILL NOT RESULT IN THE REDIRECTION OF THE SECOND OBJECT BALL. THE SECOND OBJECT BALL WILL ONLY ROLL IN THE ORIGINAL STRAIGHT LINE DIRECTION IT WAS FIRST POINTING. **YOU MUST HIT THE SIDE OF THE FIRST BALL** TO CAUSE ANY AMOUNT OF REDIRECTION OF THE SECOND OBJECT BALL.

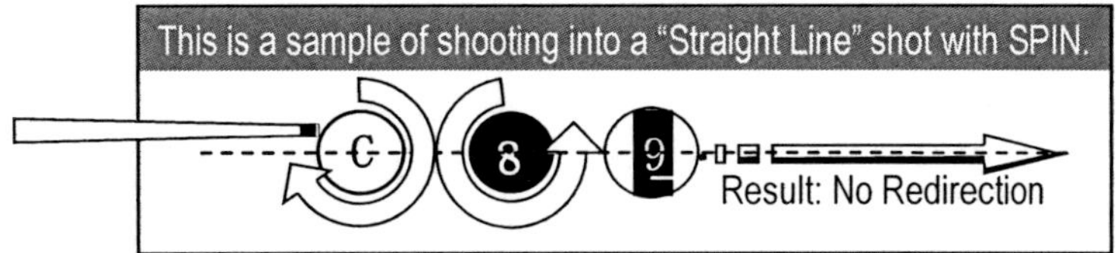

The above balls are separated for illustration purposes only. Always be sure the objet balls are frozen.

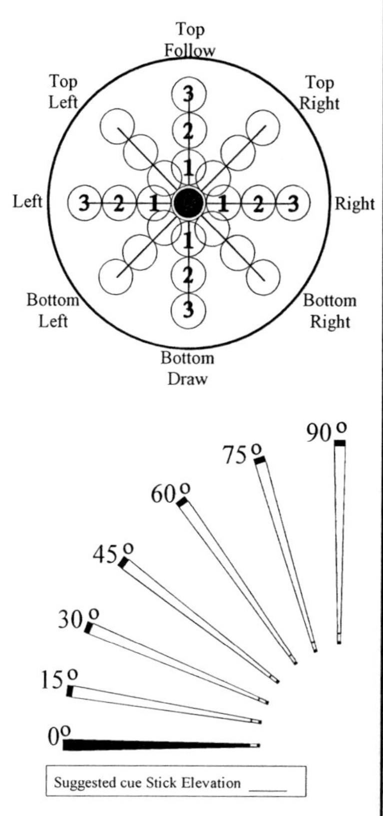

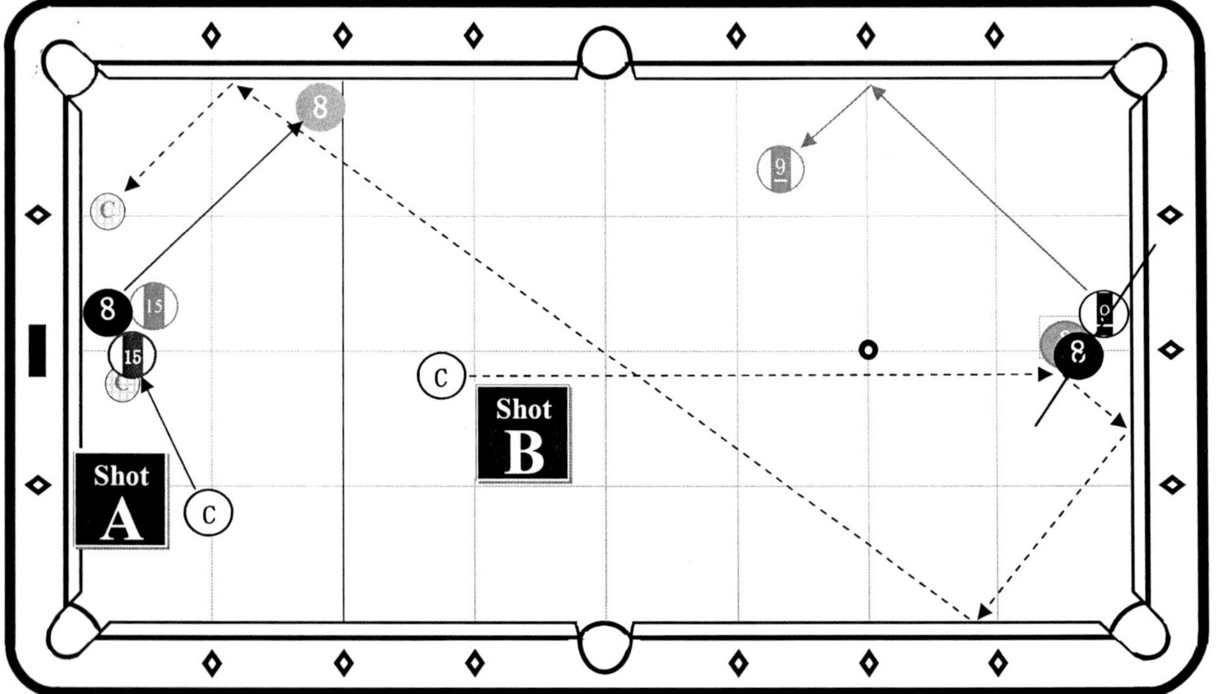

Foot Notes

Remind yourself:

"It is not required that I make a ball, every time I'm shooting, to win this game."

Remember, don't get disgusted, get defensive.

Advanced Option

Yes, you have several options. Remember to focus on the speed of only one of the balls.

PROBLEM: 1. Two object balls are close or frozen together near a rail at about a 15° to 45° angle.

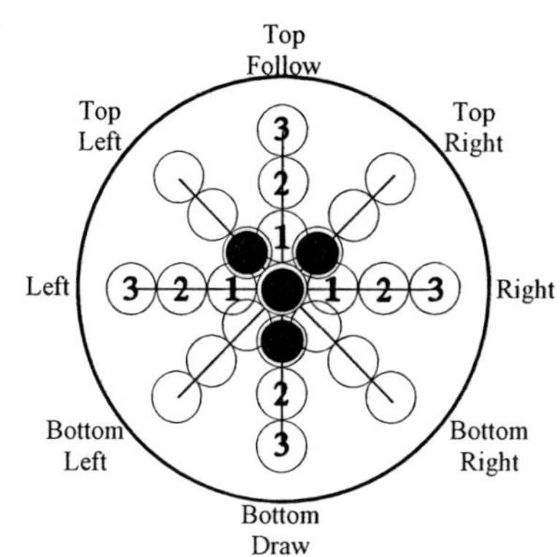

BASIC:

Shot A: A. Cue ball stays hidden behind the object ball. Drive the 8 ball to the rail, keeping the cue ball hidden behind the 15 ball.

1. Shoot directly into the 15 ball.
2. Level cue.
3. 1 Speed Stroke; enough for the 8 ball to roll to a rail and keep the cue ball hidden behind the object ball.

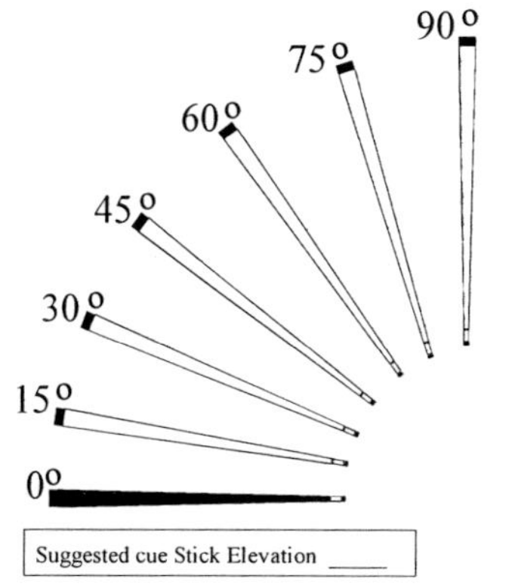

Shot B: B. Cue ball runs off the side of first ball and rolls back up the table. The ball you hit will stay in that same place.

1. Shoot on the side of the 8 ball that's in line with the 9 ball (*see the line that runs through the balls to understand this aiming point)*.
2. Level cue with your choice of applied English.
3. Use 3 or 4 Speed Stroke, but not enough to make the corner pocket.
4. Apply a smooth follow-through.

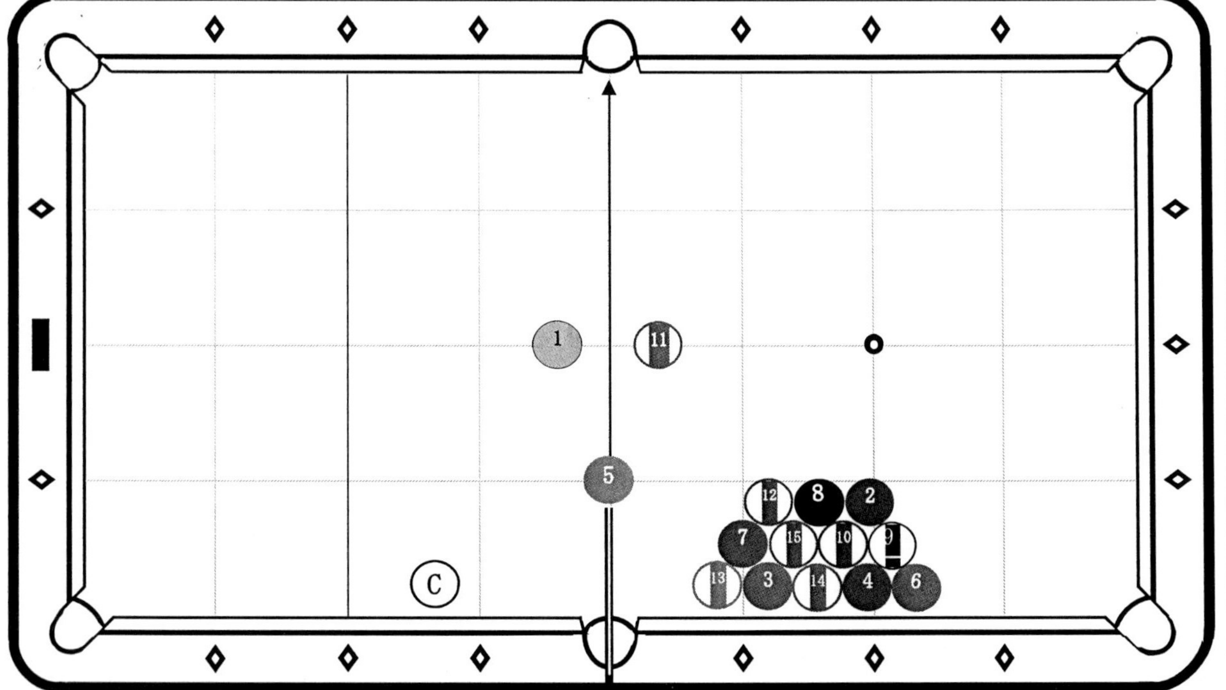

Foot Notes

When setting up the balls, line up all three balls touching in a straight line. Gently roll the center ball out with a flick of a finger.

Advanced Option Develop your aiming skills while working with these drill instructions:

1. Place a second object ball in front of the opposite side pocket.
2. Your eyes are now on the object ball at the time you shoot, not the cue ball.
3. Work on your draw stroke and off center hits.

PROBLEM: 1. The space is very close between two object balls.
2. You don't see an option to kick.
3. No Jump cues allowed or you don't have one.

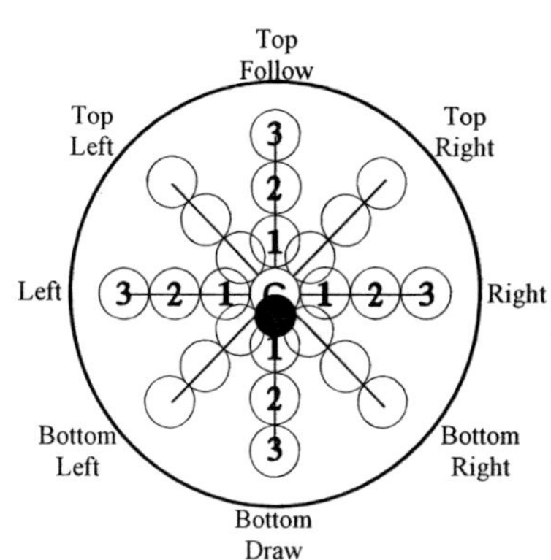

BASIC:

1. Set a full rack of balls alongside the long rail.
2. Place two object balls in the center of the table exactly one ball-width apart, as shown above.
3. Place an object ball one Diamond away in front of the two balls.
4. Elevate the butt end of your stick 15° to 30°.
5. Aim, looking directly between the two balls.
6. Strike the cue ball ½ Tip above center with a ***VERY*** loose grip.
7. Use between a 6 to 8 Speed Stroke, depending on the distance and height of the jump.

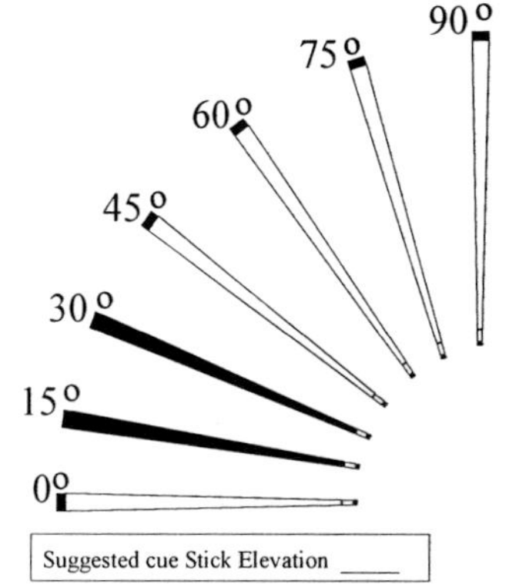

The object ball will rocket directly into the pocket without touching the other two balls.
Shoot the entire rack, including the cue ball, into the side pocket without missing. **BACK HAND IS A LOOSE AND SNAPPING STROKE**

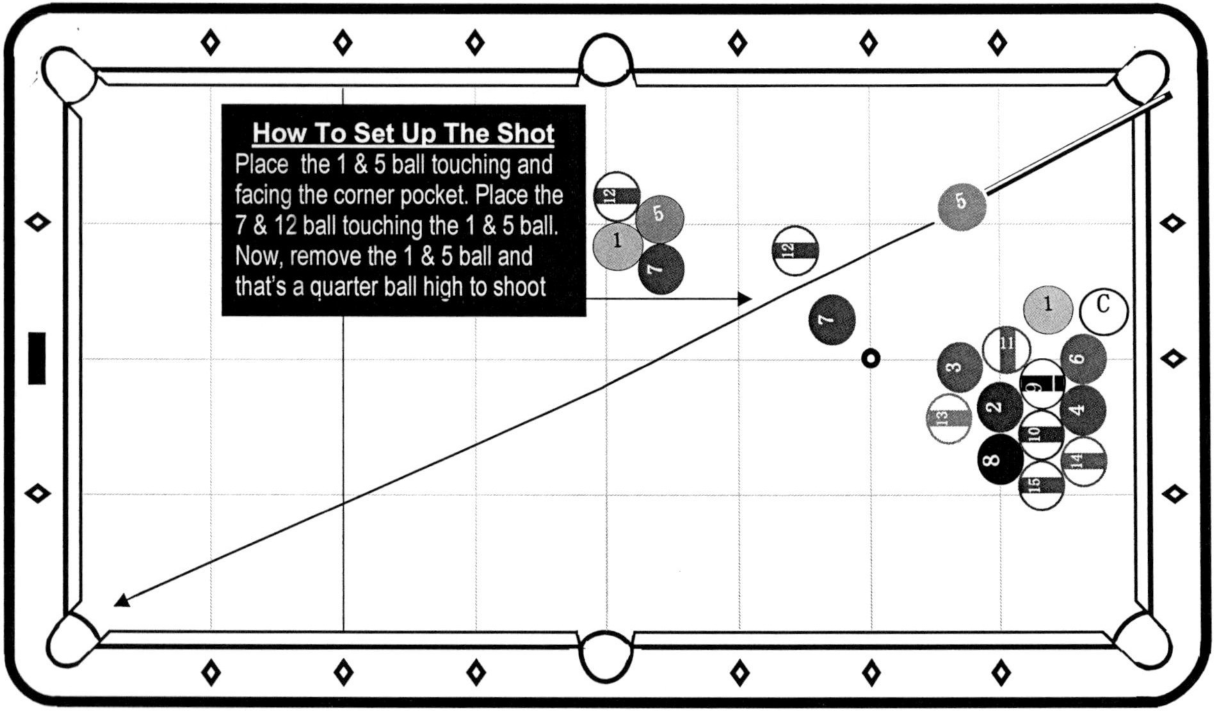

28

How To Set Up The Shot

Place the 1 & 5 ball touching and facing the corner pocket. Place the 7 & 12 ball touching the 1 & 5 ball. Now, remove the 1 & 5 ball and that's a quarter ball high to shoot

Foot Notes

This shot can work well by using a break cue because of its lighter weight and harder tip.

Advanced Option

Develop your aiming skills while working with these drill instructions

1. Place an object ball in front of the corner pocket.
2. Look at the object ball at the time you shoot.

PROBLEM: 1. Only ½ ball space between the two object balls.
2. No options to kick, you must jump.

BASIC:

1. Set a full rack of balls alongside the bottom rail.
2. Place two object balls ½ BALL APART.
3. Place an object ball 1½ Diamonds away in front of the two balls.
4. Elevate the butt end of your stick about 30°.
5. Aim directly between the two balls to align the shot with the corner pocket. At the shot release, eyes are fixed on the corner pocket.
6. Strike the cue ball firmly about ½ Tip above center with a ***VERY*** loose grip and a fast flicking stroke.

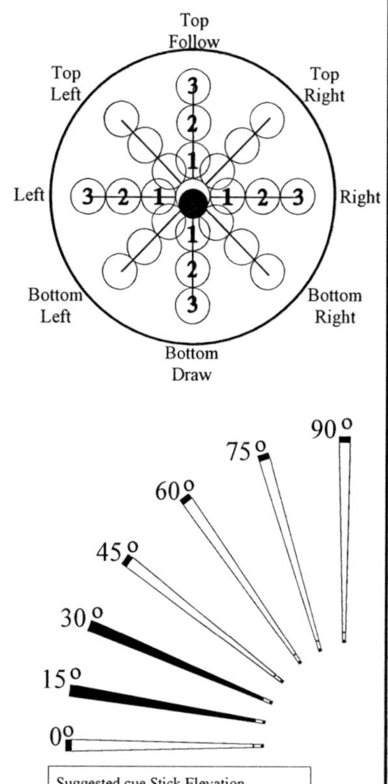

Keep a lose grip and snap your wrist when shooting. After each succesful rack, move the balls closer to learn your maximum jumping height.

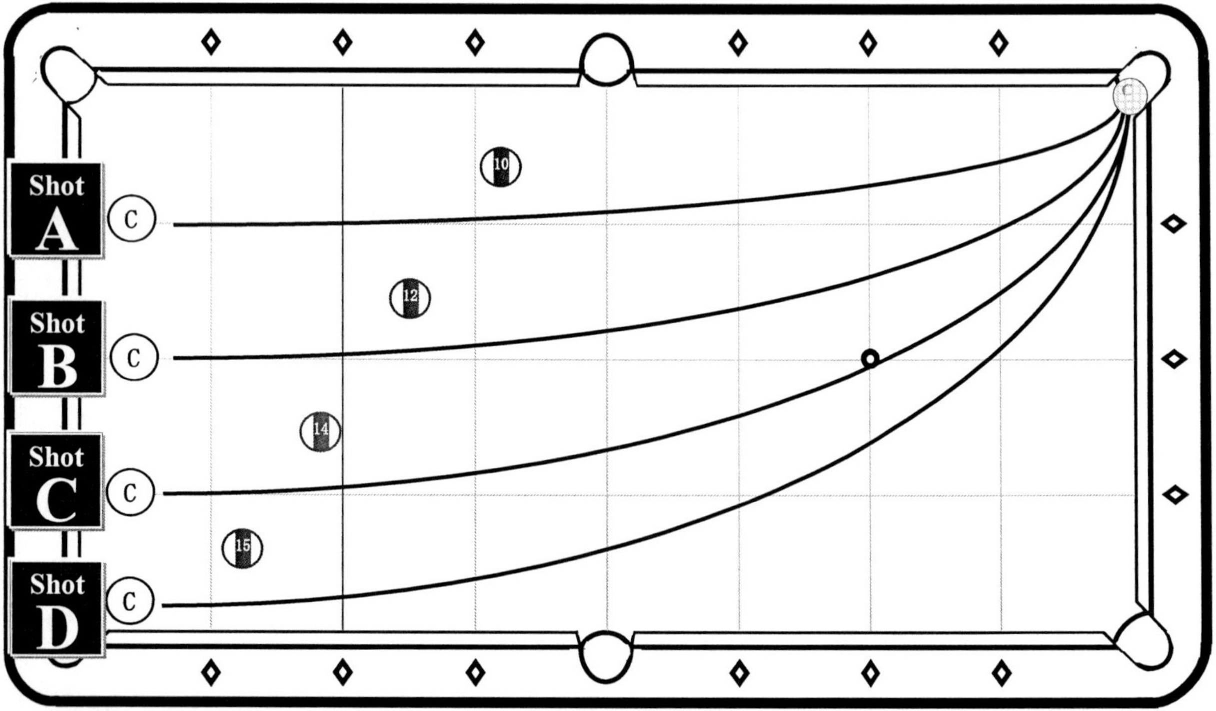

Shot A

Shot B

Shot C

Shot D

Foot Notes

2 Tips of English can be determined by turning an striped ball vertical and hitting at the outer edge of the colored stripe.

Advanced Option

1. Aim two object balls to the outside of the object ball you will curve around.
2. Any need to Massé more than two Diamonds could be classified as an artistic pool trick shot.

PROBLEM: 1. Object ball is in the direct path of your shot.
2. You don't have an option to kick or jump.

BASIC:

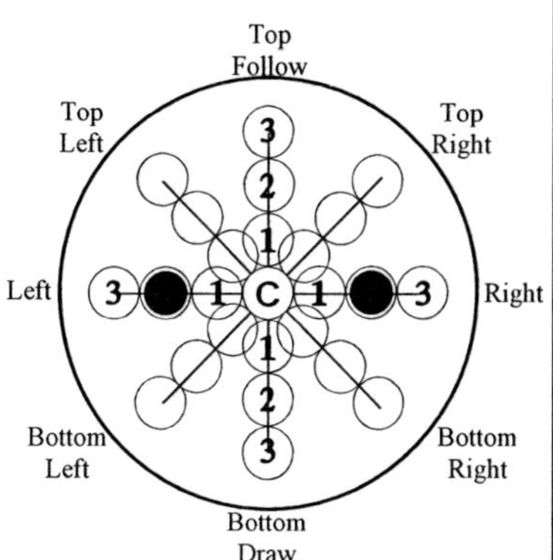

Shot A:
1. Aim at Diamond up table.
2. Elevate cue 30°.
3. 2 Tips of English.
4. 5 Speed Stroke.
5. Stroke smoothly through ball.

Shot B:
1. Aim at the Diamond up table.
2. Elevate cue 45°.
3. 2 Tips of English.
4. 5 Speed Stroke.
5. Stroke smoothly through ball.

Shot C:
1. Aim at Diamond up table.
2. Elevate cue 60°.
3. 2 Tips of English.
4. 5 Speed Stroke.
5. Stroke smoothly through ball.

Shot D:
1. Aim at the Diamond up table.
2. Elevate cue 75°.
3. 2 Tips of English.
4. 5 Speed Stroke.
5. Stroke smoothly through ball.

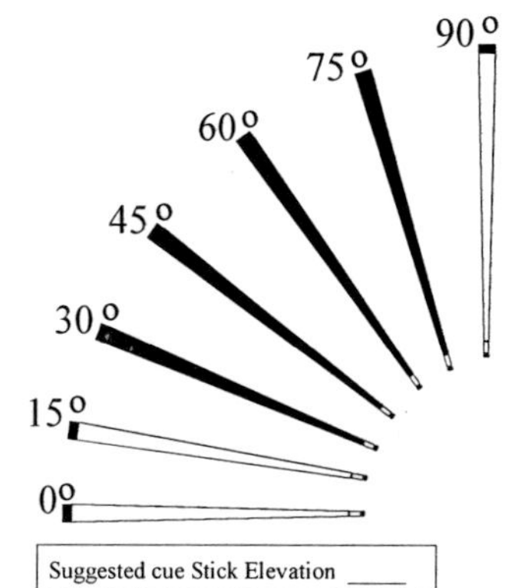

Note: Detailed lessons on Speed Strokes can be found in BOOT CAMP Volume 7.

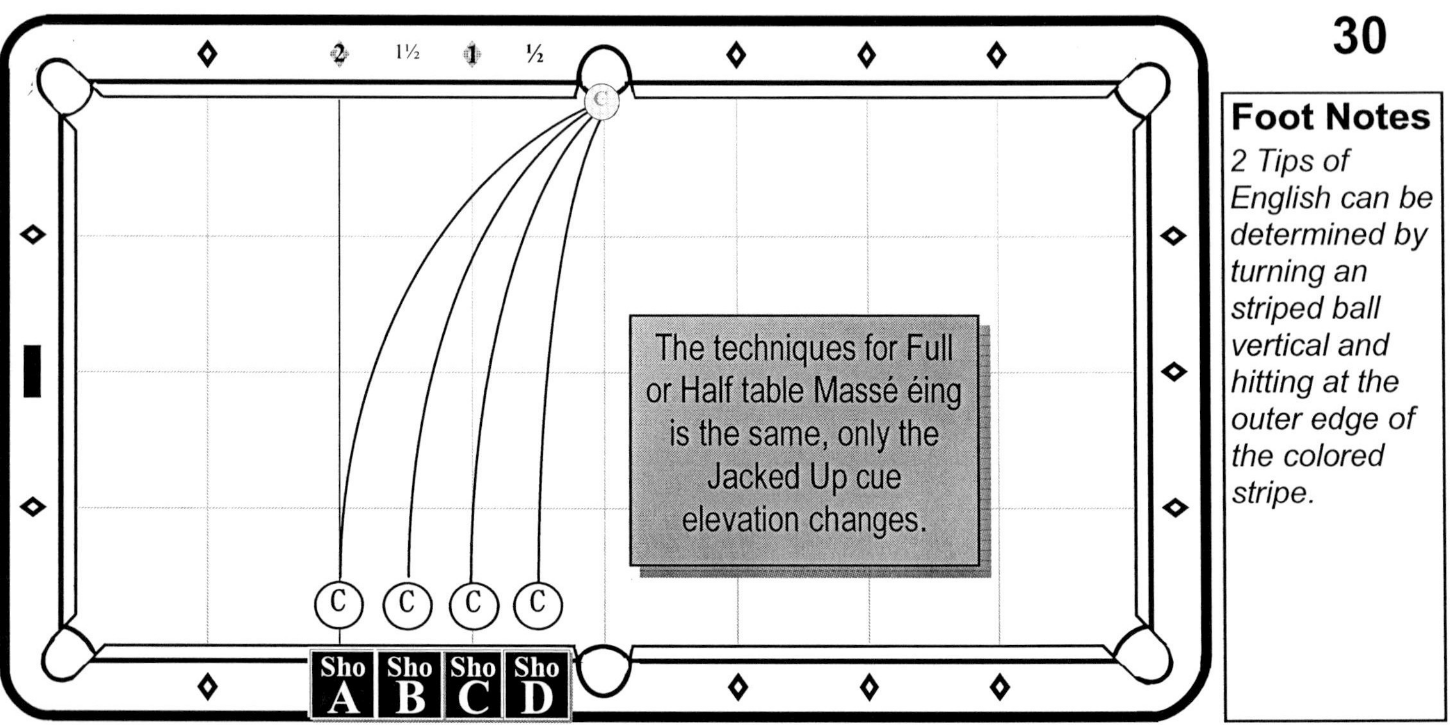

Foot Notes

2 Tips of English can be determined by turning an striped ball vertical and hitting at the outer edge of the colored stripe.

Advanced Option

Aim two full ball lengths to the outside of the object ball you intend to Massé around.

PROBLEM: 1. Object ball is in the direct path of your shot.
2. You don't have an option to kick or jump.

BASIC:

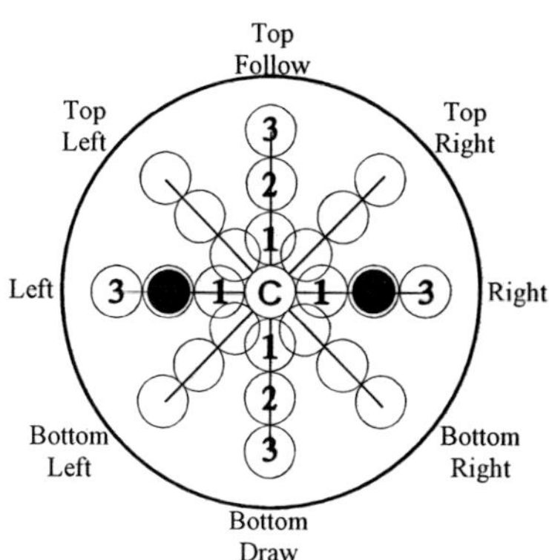

Shot A:

1. Aim from 2 Diamonds across table.
2. Elevate cue 75°.
3. 2 Tips of English.
4. 5 Speed Stroke.
5. Stroke smoothly through ball.

Shot B:

1. Aim from 1½ Diamonds across table
2. Elevate cue 60°.
3. 2 Tips of English.
4. 5 Speed Stroke.
5. Stroke smoothly through ball.

Shot C:

1. Aim from 1 Diamond across table.
2. Elevate cue 45°.
3. 2 Tips of English.
4. 5 Speed Stroke.
5. Stroke smoothly through ball.

Shot D:

1. Aim from ½ Diamond across table.
2. Elevate cue 30°.
3. 2 Tips of English.
4. 5 Speed Stroke.
5. Stroke smoothly through ball.

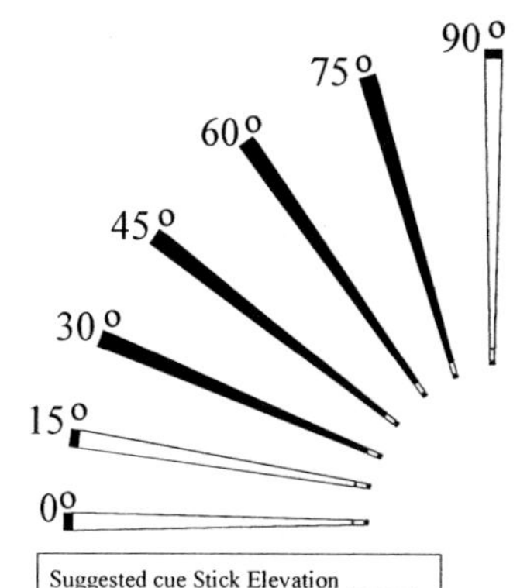

Note: Detailed lessons on Speed Strokes can be found in BOOT CAMP Volume 7

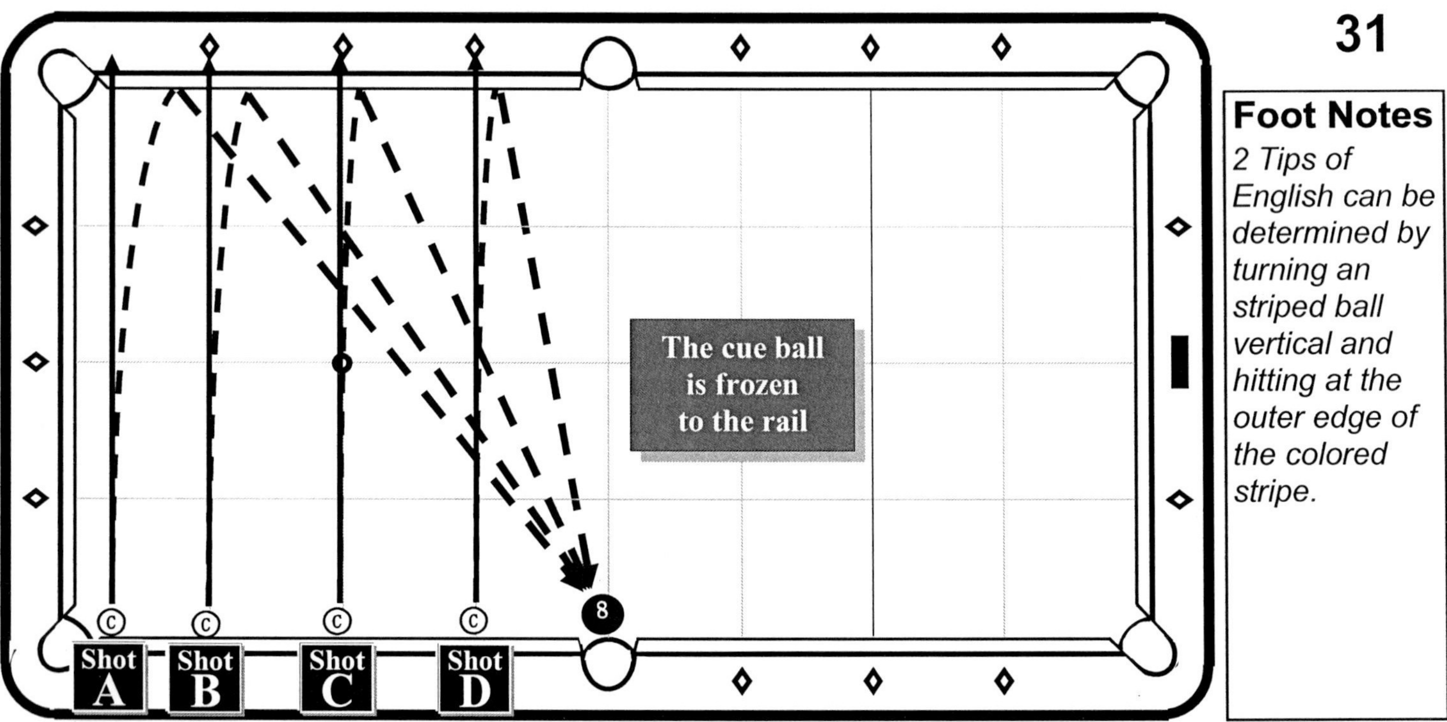

Foot Notes

2 Tips of English can be determined by turning an striped ball vertical and hitting at the outer edge of the colored stripe.

Advanced Option

Aim one full ball length to the outside of the object ball you intend to Massé around.

PROBLEM: 1. Object ball is in the direct path of your shot.
2. You don't have an option to kick or jump.

BASIC:

Shot A:
1. Aim at Rail directly across table.
2. Elevate cue 45°.
3. 2 Tips of English.
4. 5 Speed Stroke.
5. Stroke smoothly through the ball.

Shot B:
1. Aim at Diamond directly up table.
2. Elevate cue 30°.
3. 2 Tips of English.
4. 5 Speed Stroke.
5. Stroke smoothly through the ball.

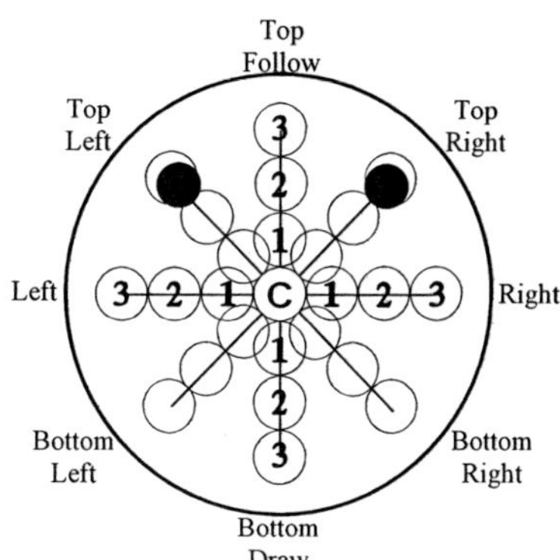

Shot C:
1. Aim at Diamond directly up table.
2. Elevate cue 15°.
3. 2 Tips of English.
4. 5 Speed Stroke.
5. Stroke smoothly through the ball.

Shot D:
1. Aim at Diamond directly up table.
2. Level cue.
3. 2 Tips of English.
4. 5 Speed Stroke.
5. Stroke smoothly through the ball.

Note: Detailed lessons on Speed Strokes can be found in BOOT CAMP Volume 7.

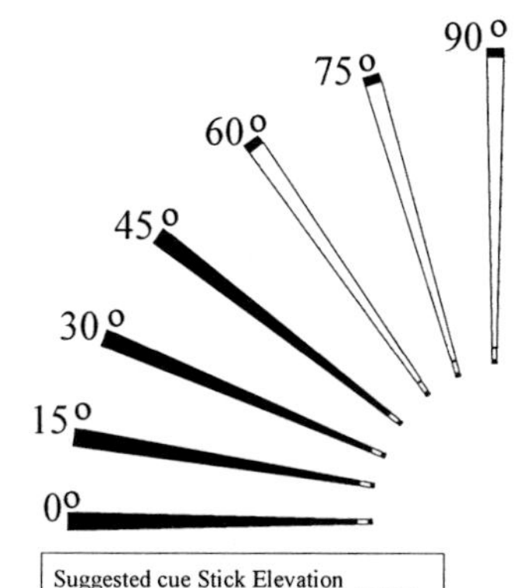

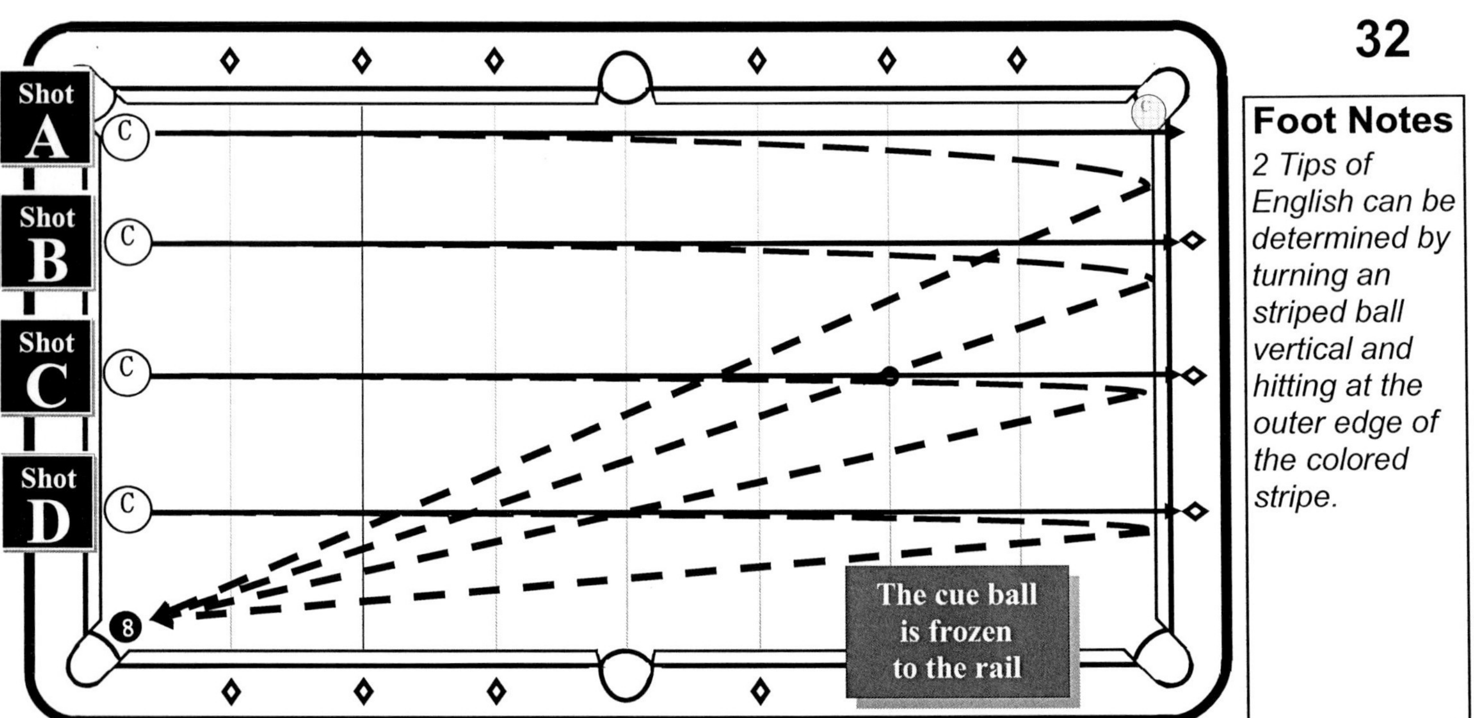

Foot Notes

2 Tips of English can be determined by turning an striped ball vertical and hitting at the outer edge of the colored stripe.

Advanced Option

Aim one full ball length to the outside of the object ball you intend to Massé around.

PROBLEM: 1. Object ball is in the direct path of your shot.
2. You don't have an option to kick or jump.

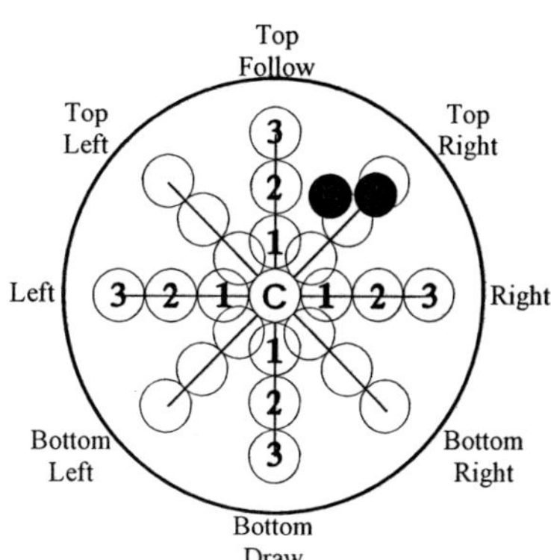

BASIC:

Shot A:
1. Aim directly up table.
2. Elevate cue 30°.
3. 2 Tips of English.
4. 5 Speed Stroke.
5. Stroke smoothly through ball.

Shot B:
1. Aim at Diamond directly up table.
2. Elevate cue 15°.
3. 2 Tips of English.
4. 5 Speed Stroke.
5. Stroke smoothly through ball.

Shot C:
1. Aim at Diamond directly up table.
2. Level cue.
3. 2 Tips of English.
4. 5 Speed Stroke.
5. Stroke smoothly through ball.

Shot D:
1. Aim at Diamond directly up table.
2. Level cue.
3. 1 Tip of English.
4. 5 Speed Stroke.
5. Stroke smoothly through ball.

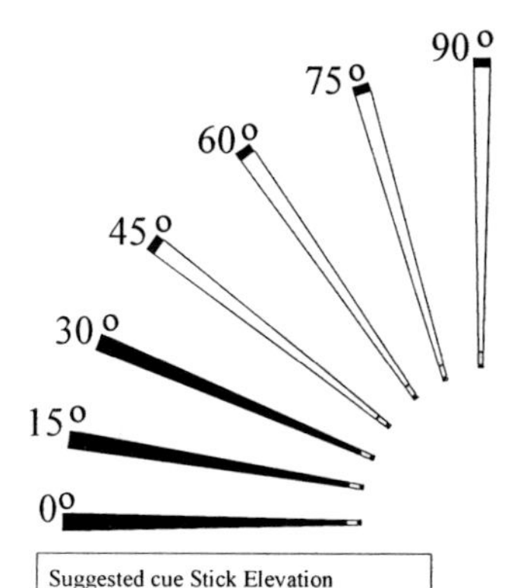

Note: Detailed lesson on the 10 Speed Strokes can be found in BOOT CAMP Volume 7.

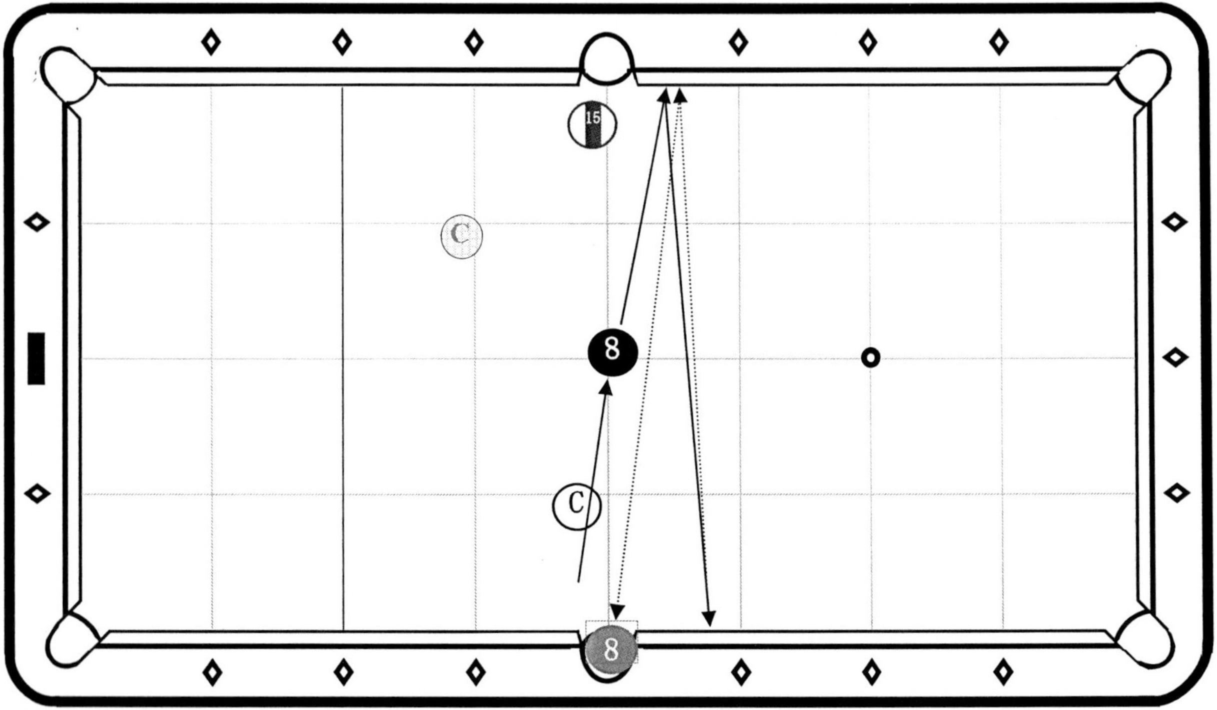

Foot Notes

This is not a lucky shot - it only looks lucky.
You call the 8 ball in the same side pocket as you are standing by.

Advanced Option

Remember the English Rule: Whichever side of the side pocket the object ball hits the first rail, apply the side SPIN English to that same side of the cue ball.

PROBLEM: 1. Side pocket is blocked for a straight in shot.

BASIC:

1. Use 2 Tips of right English (when banking to the rail on the right side of the side pocket as shown above).
   (Reverse to Left side English if banking to the rail to the left side of the side pocket).
2. Shoot into the rail about 4 inches past the side pocket.
3. Use a 6 to 8 speed stroke (test this shot before match to prove the rail).
4. Use a smooth level follow-through stroke.

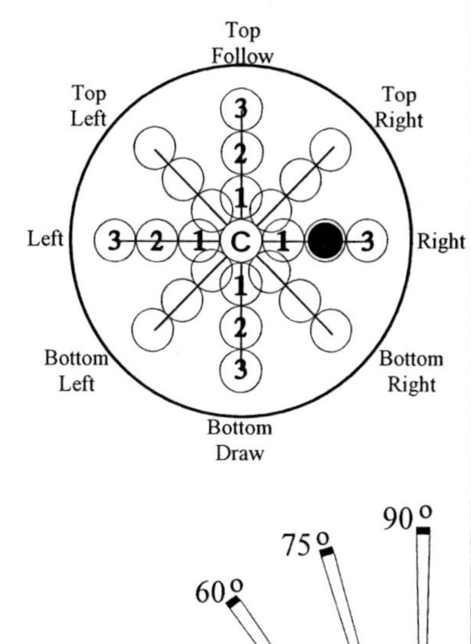

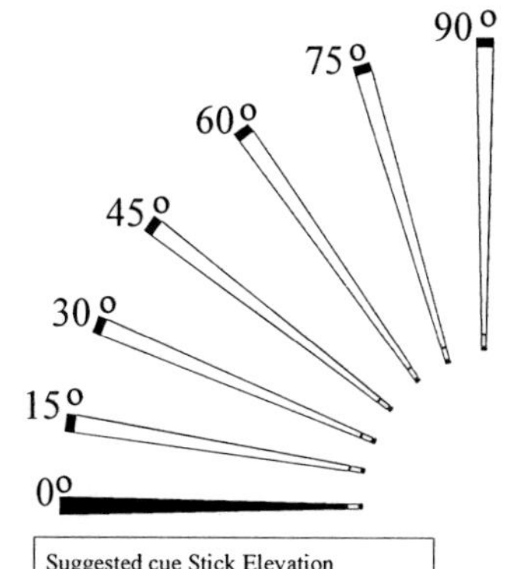

33 DOUBLE BACK BANK SHOT

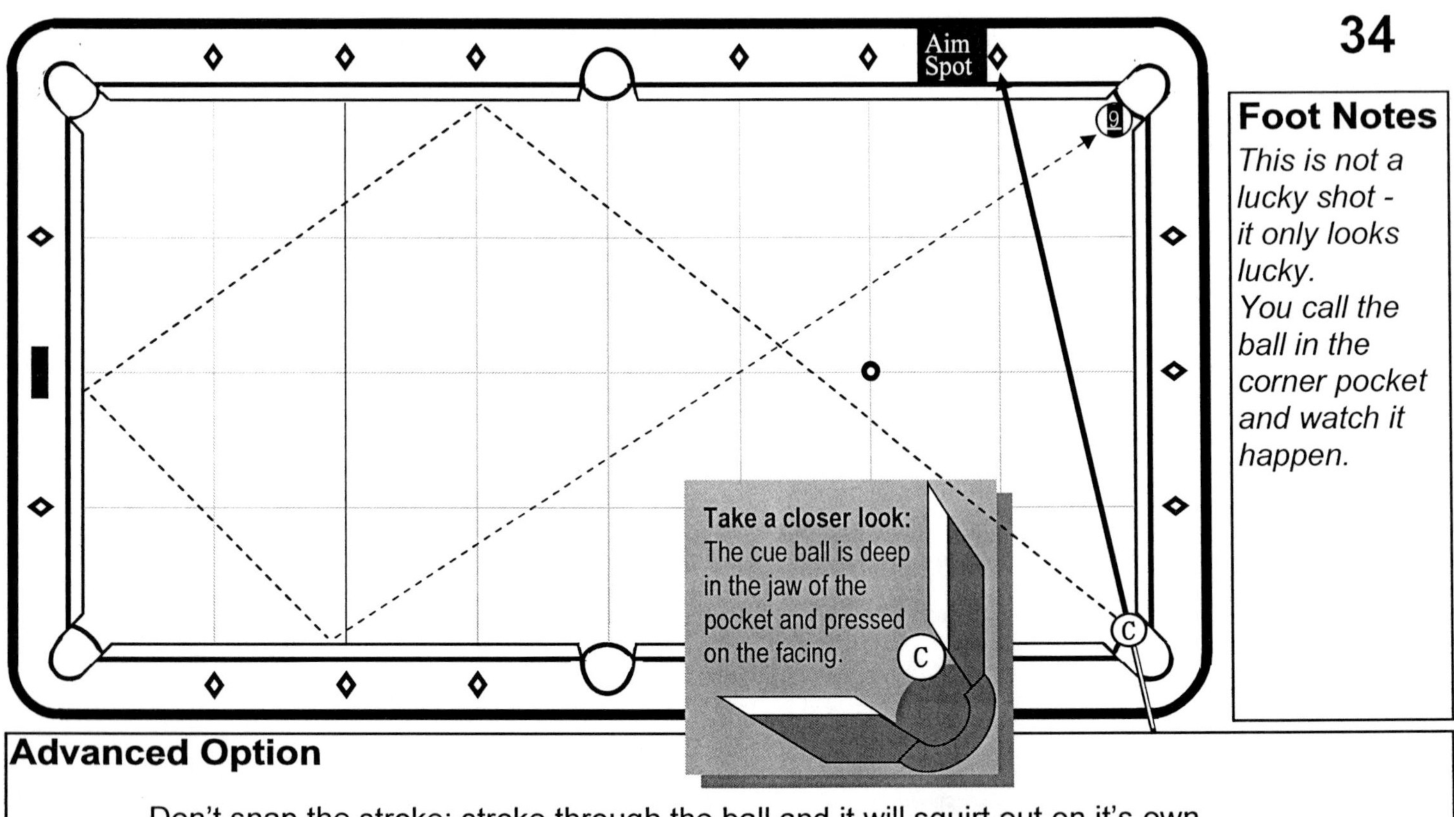

Foot Notes

This is not a lucky shot - it only looks lucky. You call the ball in the corner pocket and watch it happen.

Advanced Option

Don’t snap the stroke; stroke through the ball and it will squirt out on it’s own.

PROBLEM: 1. Cue ball is frozen to the inside shim of the pocket.

BASIC:

1. Aim directly at the first Diamond across the table. (see the solid black line above).
2. Hit the center of the cue ball.
3. Use a 6 to 7 speed stroke.
4. Poke the cue ball (no follow-through).

NOTE: It really matters if the cue ball is frozen to that inside shim. Make sure it is.

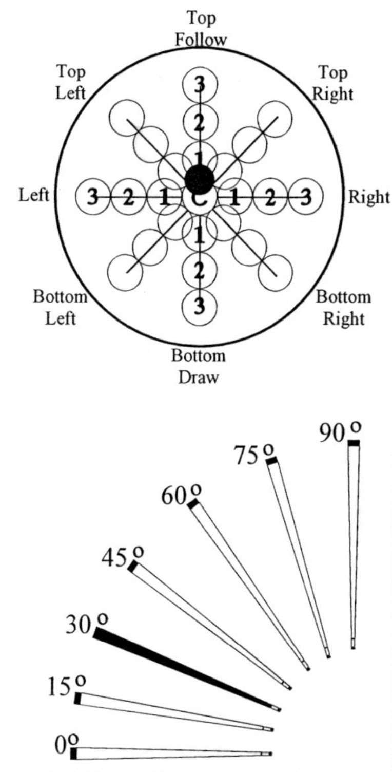

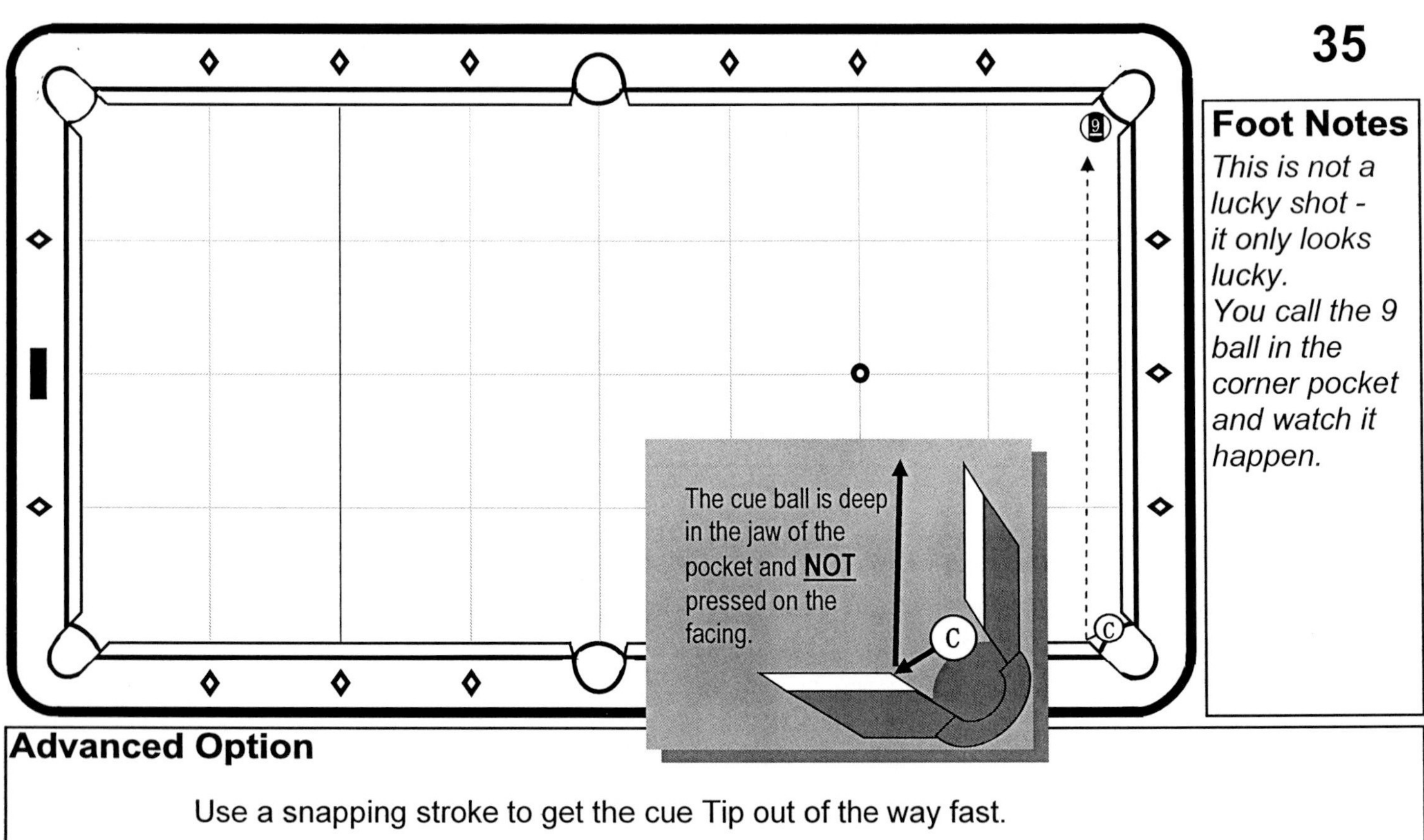

Foot Notes

This is not a lucky shot - it only looks lucky. You call the 9 ball in the corner pocket and watch it happen.

Advanced Option

Use a snapping stroke to get the cue Tip out of the way fast.

PROBLEM: 1. Cue ball is deep inside the shim of the pocket.

BASIC:

1. Determine that the balls are definitely frozen together.
2. Shoot with a level cue as best as possible.
3. Hit as close to the center of the cue ball without hitting the object ball.
4. Use a 3 to 4 speed stroke.
5. Short stroke the cue ball (no follow-through).

Top Follow
Top Left
Top Right
Left
Right
Bottom Left
Bottom Right
Bottom Draw
3 2 1 C 1 2 3

90º
75º
60º
45º
30º
15º
0º

Suggested cue Stick Elevation ____

Don't assume this is just a simple trick shot. Work on it until you have made it 25 times and when it actually happens to you, you'll feel confident you can make it happen.

35 NOT FROZEN INSIDE THE POCKET

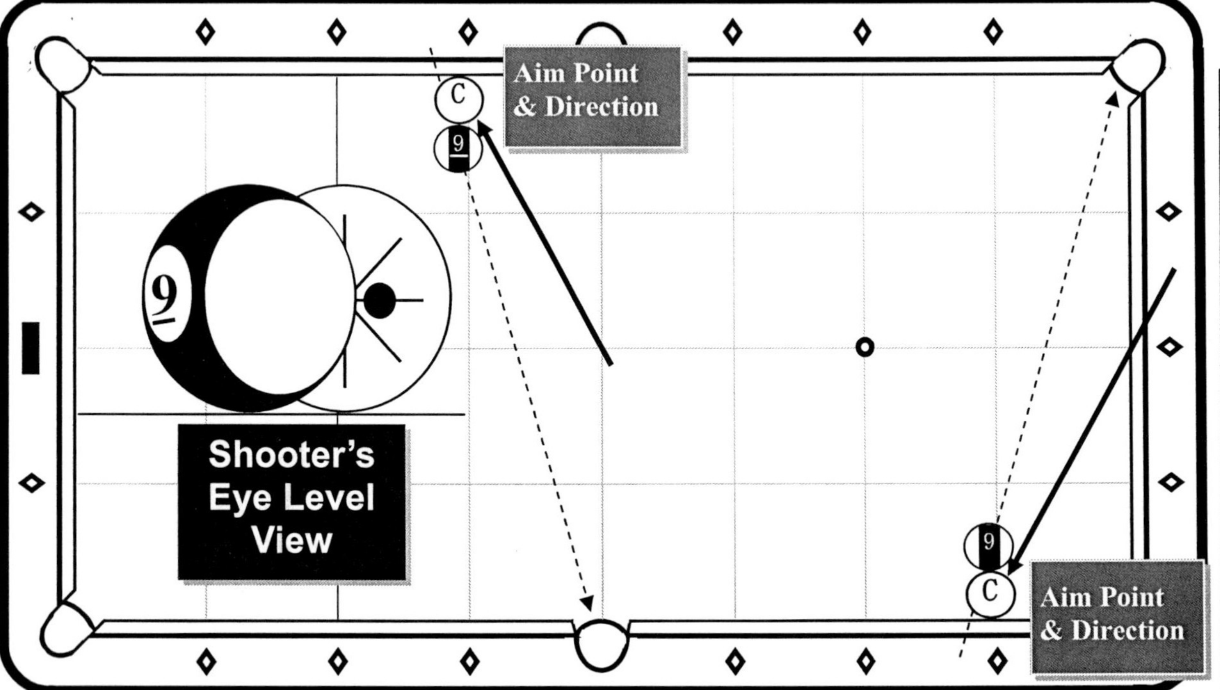

Foot Notes

The cue ball will first press into the rail, then spring out of the rail at the needed angle to hit the object ball at the proper aiming spot, to cut it toward the desired direction.

Advanced Option

When playing a lesser experienced player, floating the cue ball to the short rail could result in your opponent having to shoot off the rail and end up jawing the cue ball in the corner pocket.

PROBLEM: 1. Cue ball is frozen to a rail and an object ball is frozen against it.

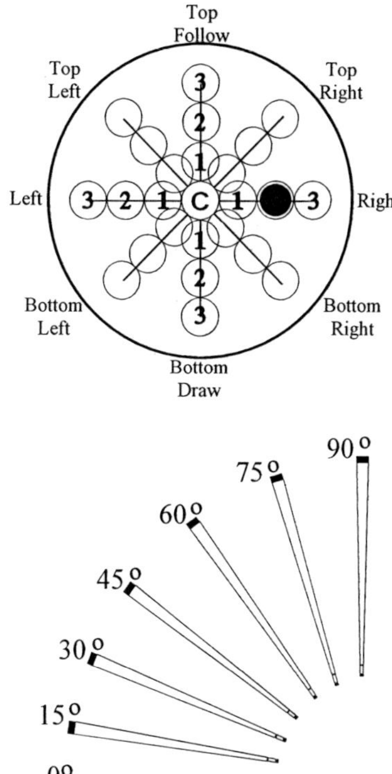

BASIC:

1. First you must be sure that the balls are frozen together.
2. Shoot with a level cue as best as possible.
3. The shaft of your cue stick should be as close to the object ball as possible while hitting the object ball 2 Tips from the center of the cue ball.
4. Use a 3 to 4 speed stroke.
5. Use a smooth stroke through the cue ball.

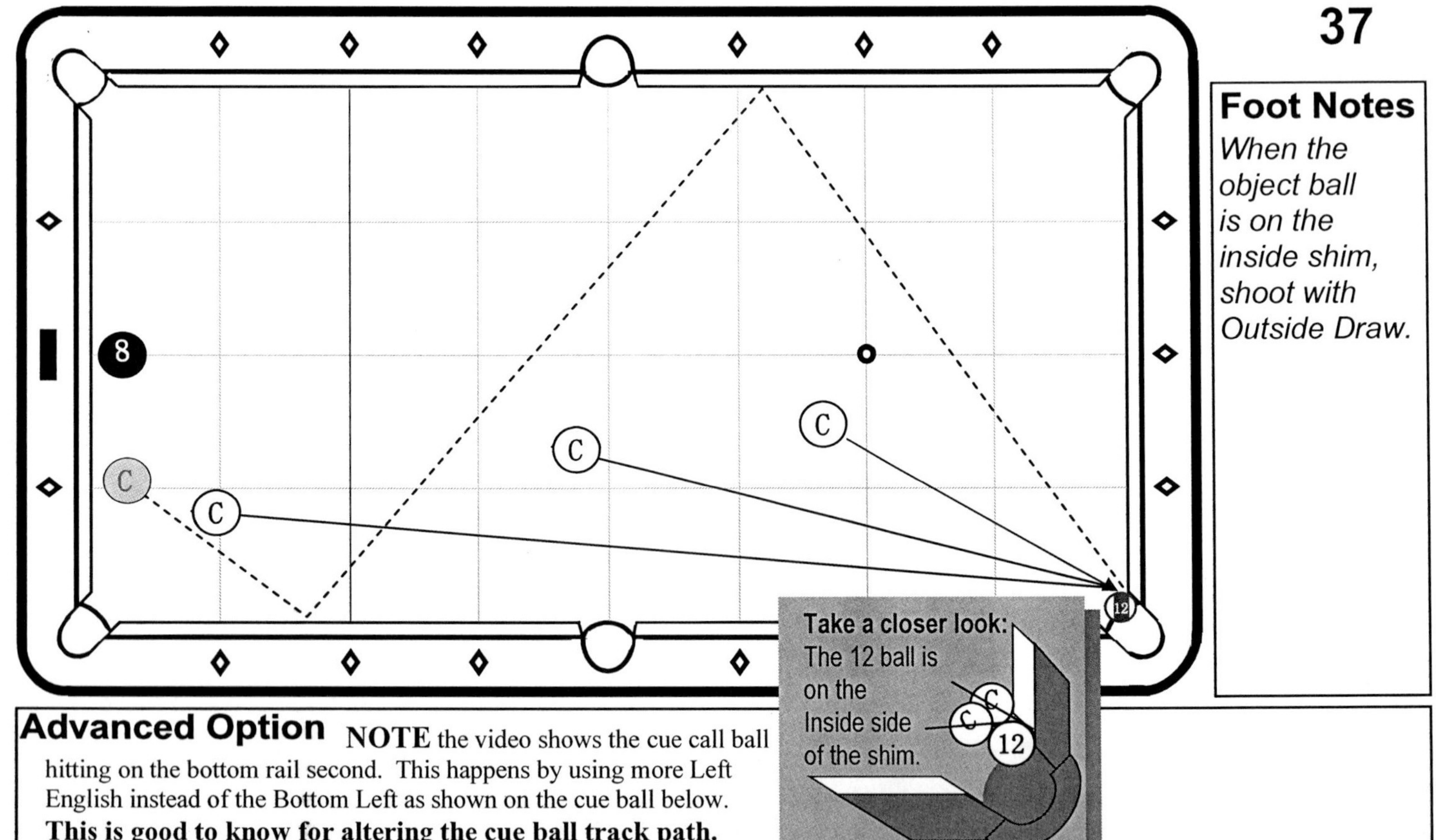

Foot Notes

When the object ball is on the inside shim, shoot with Outside Draw.

Advanced Option **NOTE** the video shows the cue call ball hitting on the bottom rail second. This happens by using more Left English instead of the Bottom Left as shown on the cue ball below. **This is good to know for altering the cue ball track path.**

PROBLEM: 1. Object ball is in the jaw - near the INSIDE shim.
2. You need to get position for the 8 ball next.

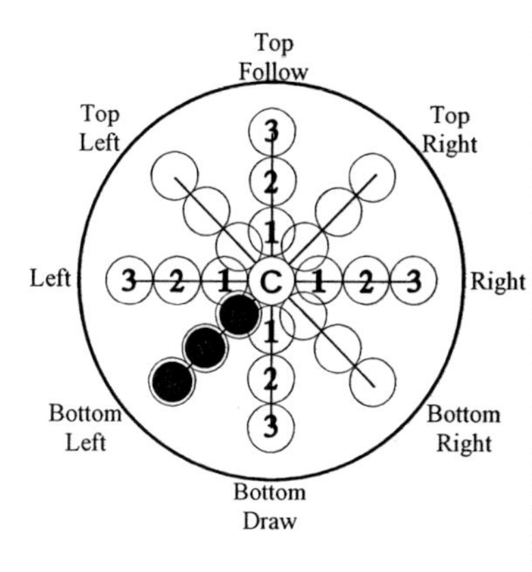

BASIC:

Object Ball is on the Inside (short rail) Side Facing.

1. Aim directly for a ½ ball hit (as shown above).
2. Level cue as best as possible with Low (Draw) English.
3. Use a 4 to 6 Speed Stroke.

NOTE: Base the Stroke Speed on the closeness of the cue ball to the object ball. Use the same speed that would return the cue ball to the bottom rail.
If the cue ball is at half table or closer, a 2 or 3 speed should do. Adjust speed more or less, based on the overall distances.

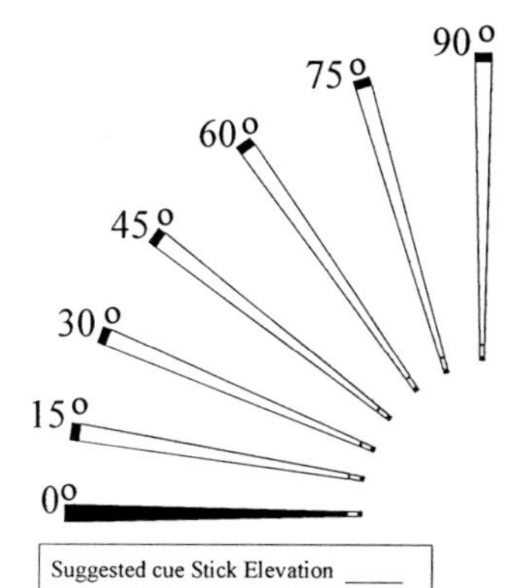

 OBJECT BALL IN THE JAW—INSIDE

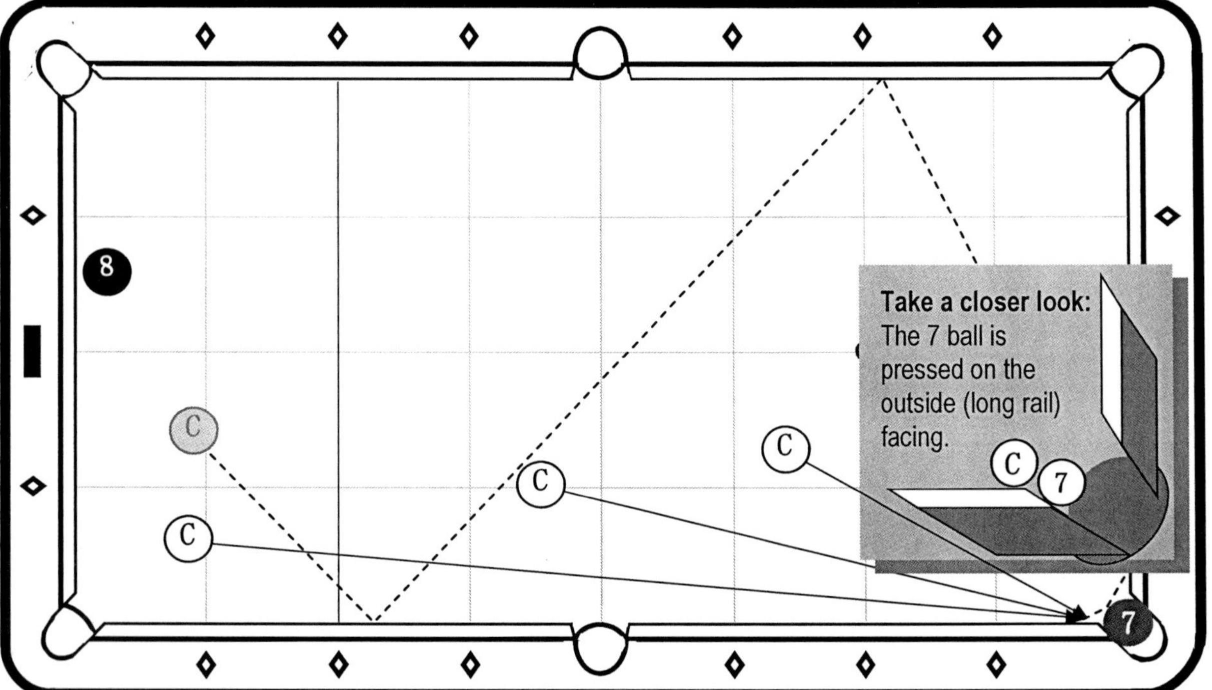

Foot Notes

Hit the side rail first about 2 inches in front of the object ball with Running English.

Advanced Option

Use Center Left to Bottom Left English to cause the cue ball to run higher into the opposite side rail if you need to get around another ball or to cross center table higher.

PROBLEM: 1. Object ball is in the jaw - near the OUTSIDE shim.
2. You need to get position for the 8 ball next.

BASIC:

Object Ball is on the Outside (long rail) Side Facing.

1. Cue ball simultaneously hits the rail and object ball.
2. Level cue as best as possible and use Running English.
3. Use 2 to 4 speed stroke.

NOTE: Base the Stroke Speed on the closeness of the cue ball to the object ball. Use the same speed that would return the cue ball to the bottom rail.
If the cue ball is at half table or closer, a 2 or 3 speed should do. Adjust speed more or less, based on the overall distances.

Be mindful that sometimes the return track of the cue ball could be right into the corner pocket. Thus, control your speed.

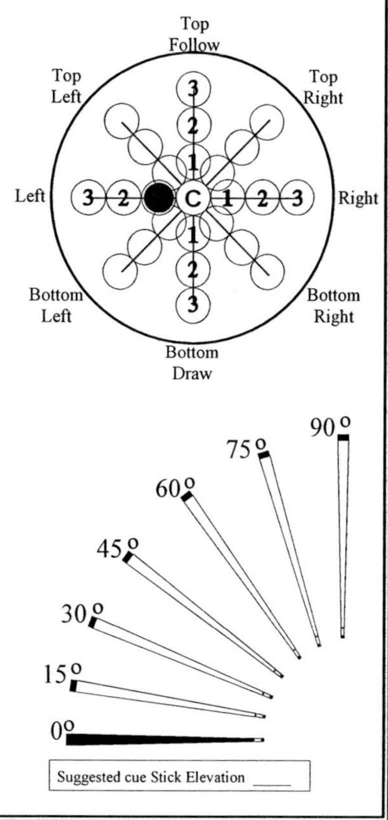

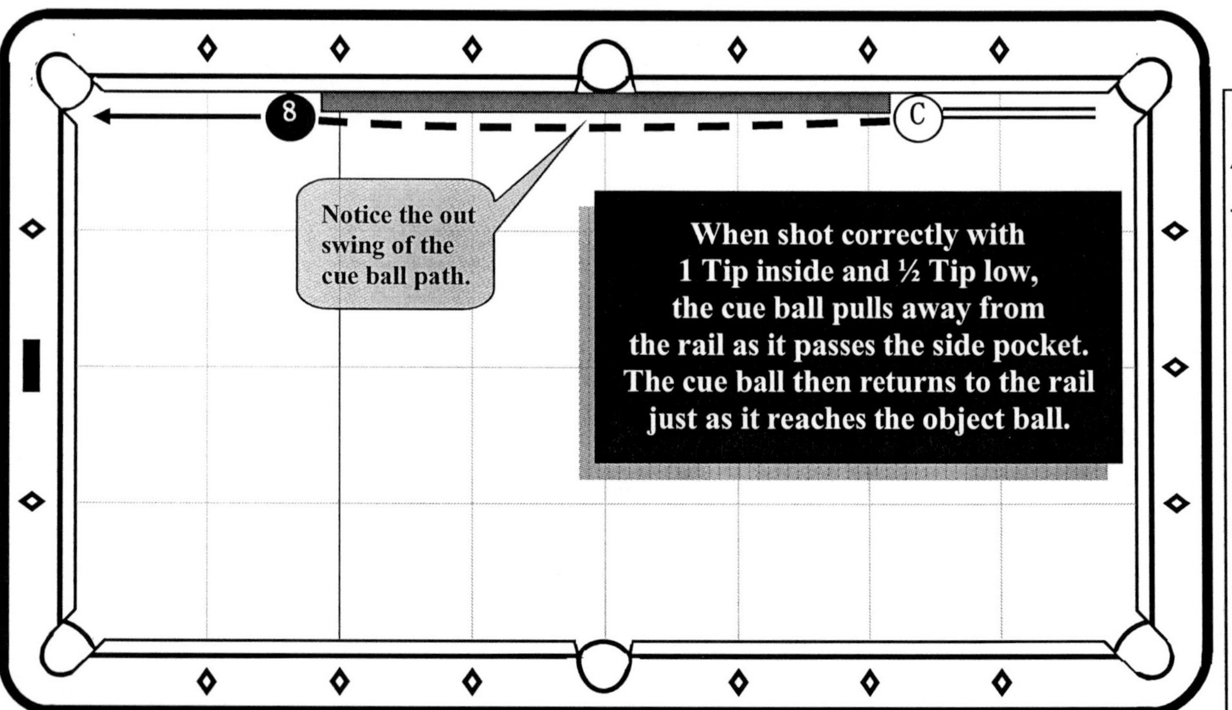

Foot Notes

Always apply your English on the side closest to the rail.

Most likely you'll use an open bridge for this shot so be sure to stroke through the cue ball smoothly and gently, but with authority.

Advanced Option

1. An ⅛ ball hit with Running English plays a great safe.
2. Shoot to the bottom rail first and kick the 8 ball back up to the top rail.

PROBLEM: 1. Object ball and cue ball are frozen on the side rail.
2. You want to shoot the 8 ball in the corner to win.

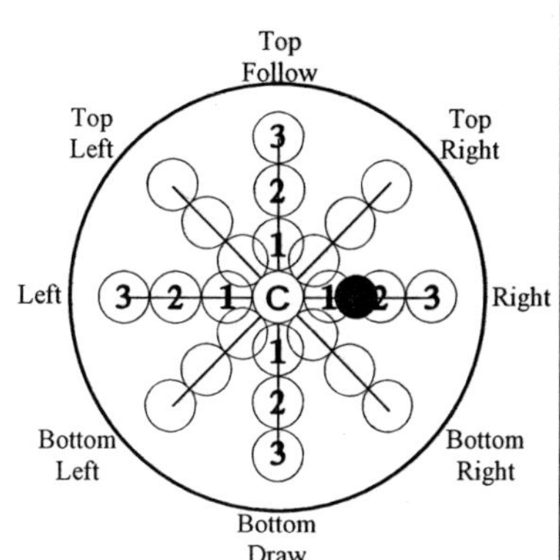

BASIC:

1. Aim straight at the object ball.
2. Apply 1½ Tip Inside.
3. Use a 2 or 3 Speed Stroke.

Basically, the cue ball will move away from the rail just enough to bypass the side pocket and curve back in to hit the object ball squarely to pocket it.

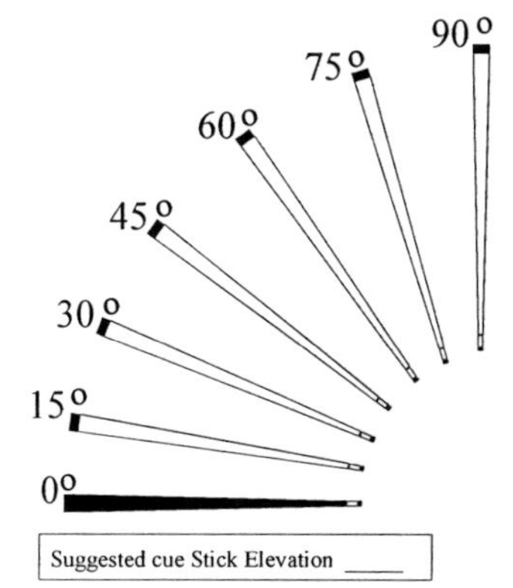

One of the most perplexing phenomena in pool is this: How does the point of the long rail, at the side pocket, stick out so much that it can poke the cue ball when it goes by?

SHOOTING PAST THE SIDE POCKET

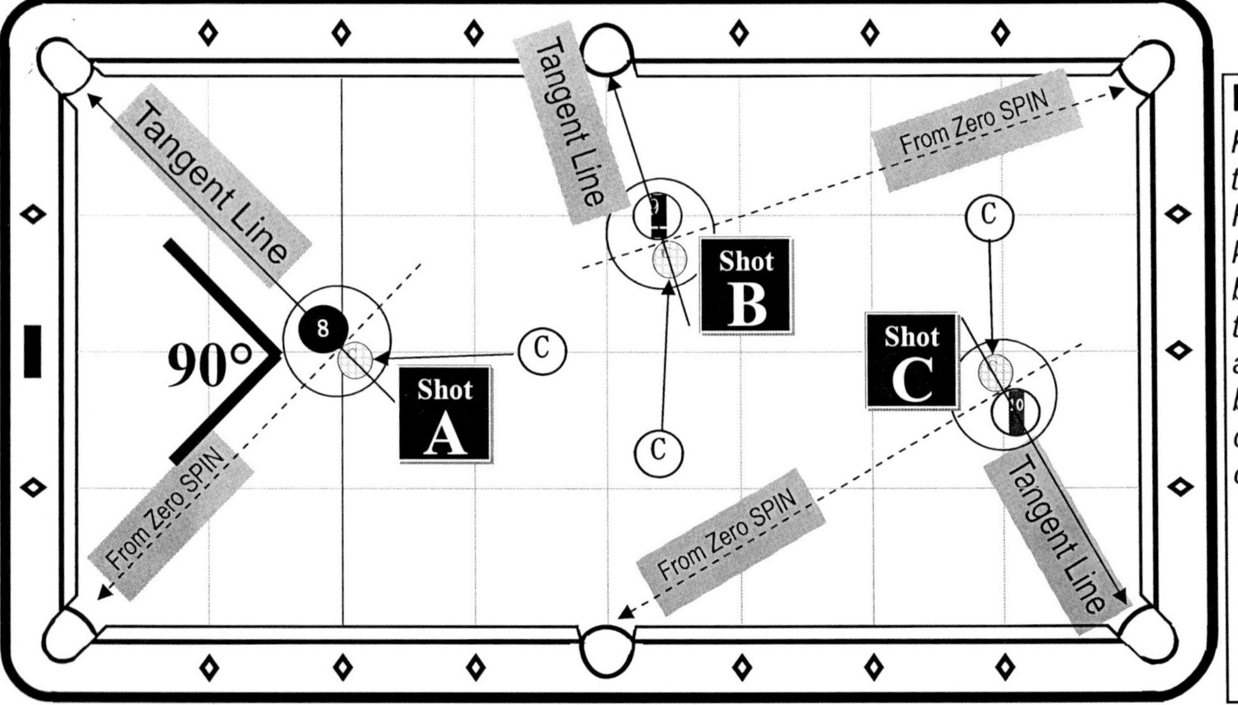

Foot Notes

Knowing how to see the 90° Rule, you can know the cue ball path after the hit and avoid a cue ball scratch on common cut shots.

Advanced Option

You can create Zero SPIN with slower speed shots by using a draw stroke to pull the cue ball to a stop at the time it reaches the object ball.

PROBLEM: 1. You have a cut shot but don't know if you will scratch.

BASIC:

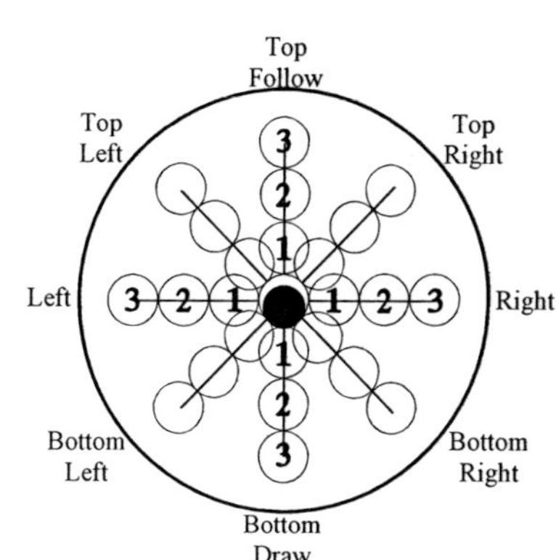

1. Object ball will be pocketed when the cue ball strikes that object ball directly on the point where the two balls become perfectly aligned to the pocket (as seen in the three circles above).

2. The path the object ball travels on is called the Tangent Line.

3. The path the cue ball travels on is called the Cue Ball Path.

4. When the cue ball contacts the object ball with **ZERO SPIN**, (Center English), it caroms off that object ball at exactly 90° from the Tangent Line.

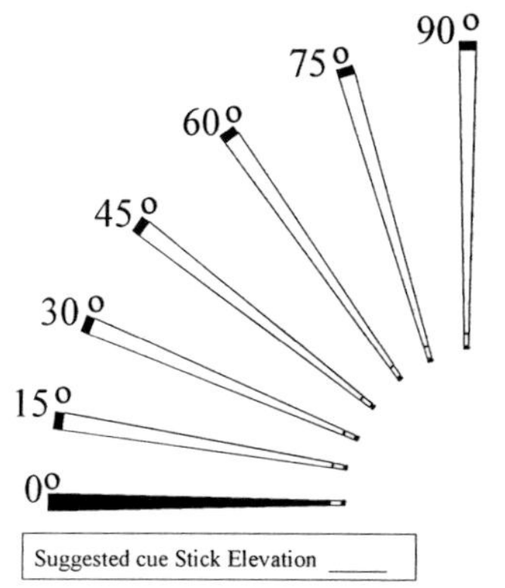

Use your cue stick or do this by sight. Place your cue stick at the back of the object ball's tangent line at a square, 90° angle. This shows you the cue ball path after the cue ball hits the object ball with ZERO SPIN. If the path looks like the cue ball will scratch, apply Top or Draw English to Open or Close the cue ball path. Set up each of the shots and attempt to cause the scratch, and then apply top or Draw English, pocketing the object ball and avoiding the cue ball scratch.

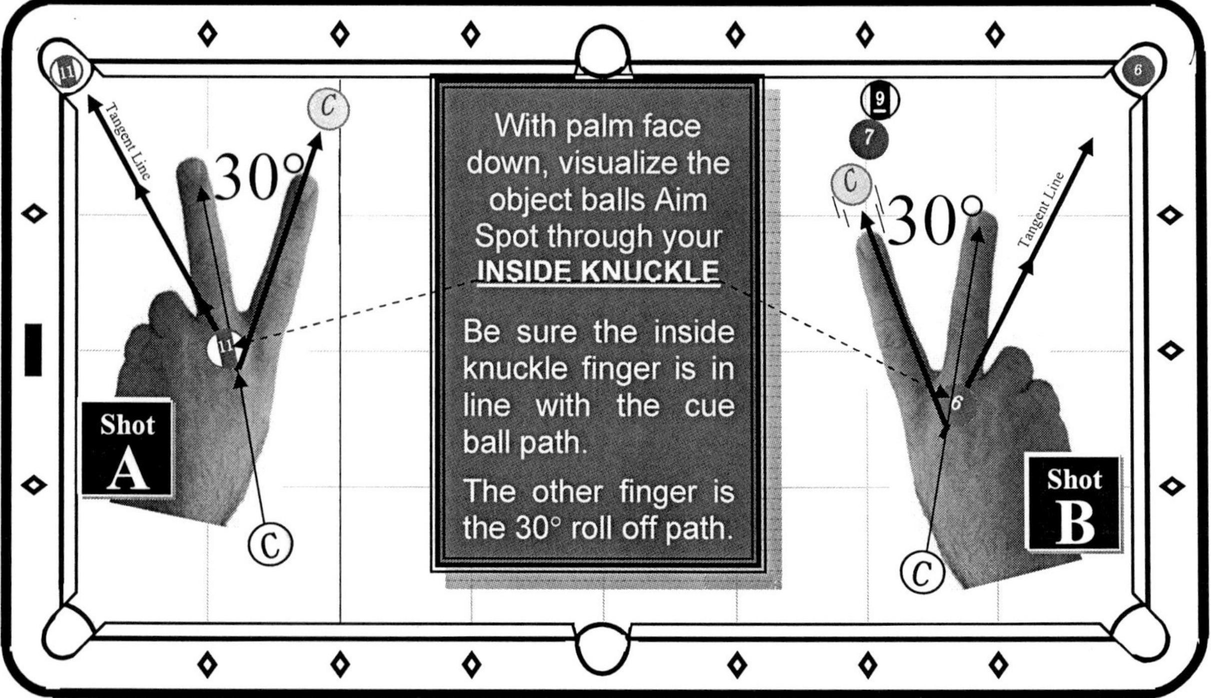

Foot Notes

The Peace sign with your fingers makes a 30° spread. Apply the 30° Rule and you will know the direction which the cue ball will roll after it contacts an object ball.

Advanced Option

1. Use Follow to close the angle more than 30°
2. Use Draw to Open the angle more than 30°

PROBLEM: 1. Don't know what direction the cue ball will roll after the first object ball has been contacted by the cue ball.

When the cue ball hits into the object ball with a **NATURAL ROLL** it will carom off that object ball's Tangent Line at exactly 30° from that Aim Spot.

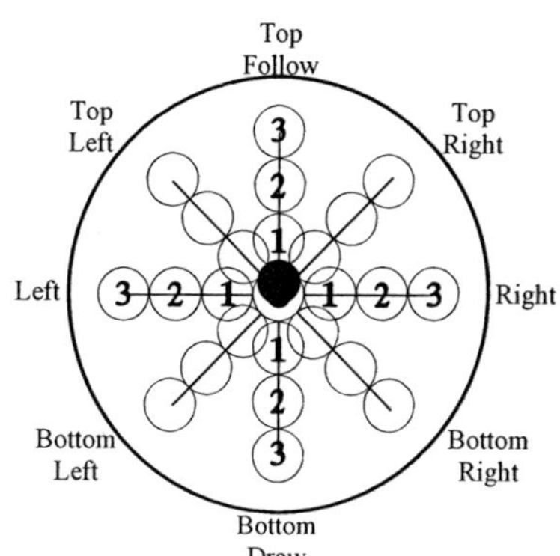

BASIC:

1. After the cue ball makes contact with the object ball, with no applied SPIN, the cue ball will roll off at a 30° angle.
2. The distance the cue ball will roll, after contacting the object ball, is based on how much Speed Stroke has been applied at the time of shooting.
3. The line the object ball travels on is called the Tangent Line.
4. Follow or Draw SPIN, at the time of contact, will alter the 30° natural roll off direction of the cue ball after contacting the cue ball.

Using either hand, spread your index and middle finger into a peace sign. Point one finger along the cue ball path at the AIMING SPOT on the object ball. The other finger will point off that path at a 30° angle. This technique shows you the cue ball path after the cue ball hits the object ball with NATURAL ROLL.

If the path looks like the cue ball will scratch, apply Top or Draw English to Open or Close the cue ball path. Set up each of the shots and attempt to cause the scratch, and then apply top or Draw English, pocketing the object ball and avoiding the cue ball scratch.

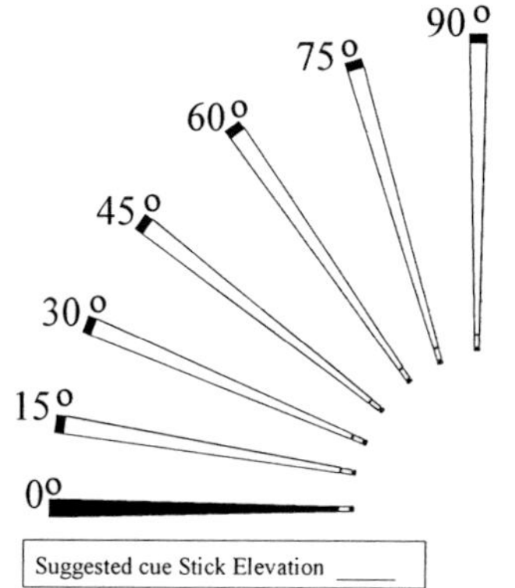

41 THE 30° RULE

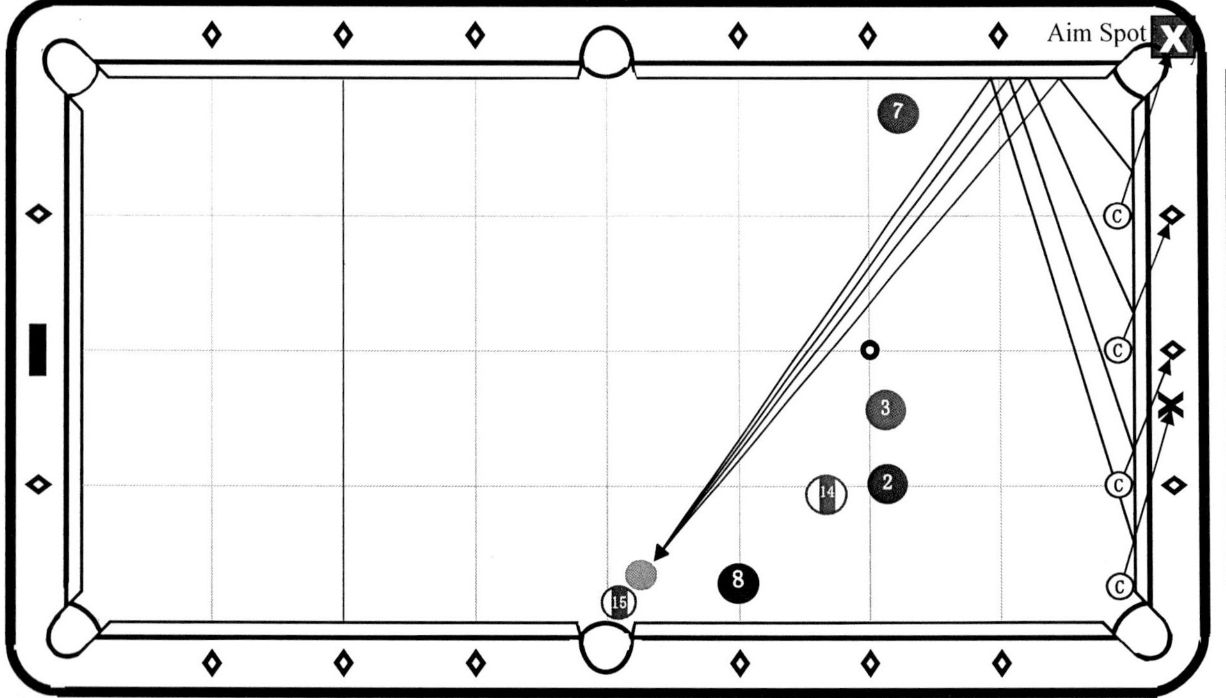

Foot Notes

Keep a positive Attitude!

Look at this shot and say,

"I love this shot!
This is my favorite shot!"

Then shoot it with authority.

Advanced Option

1. Rail plays LONG: Draw will open the angle out of the rails.
2. Rail plays SHORT: Top will close the angle out of the rails.

PROBLEM: 1. Cue ball is frozen to the short rail.
2. No clean kick or jump shot open.

BASIC:

Step 1. Be sure cue ball is frozen to the rail in front of the Diamond.

Step 2. Aim directly at the Diamond Aiming Spot (Memorize them).

Step 3. Use a level cue stroke.

Step 4. Shoot with a 3 to 5 Speed Stroke.

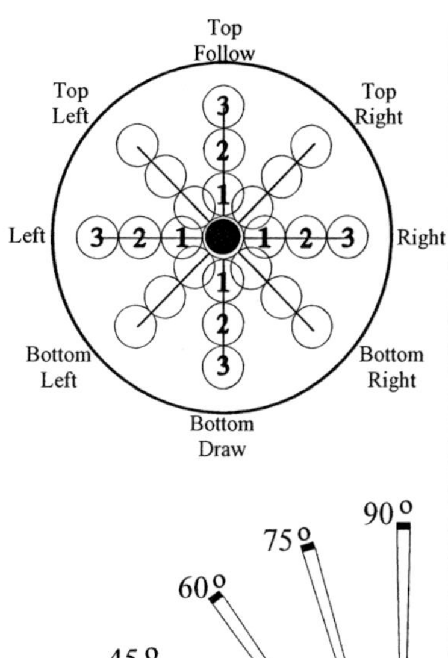

Test the rails with one of these shots before the match to determine if they will play long or short.

If the cue ball is not frozen, you have to be careful not to double hit the cue ball.

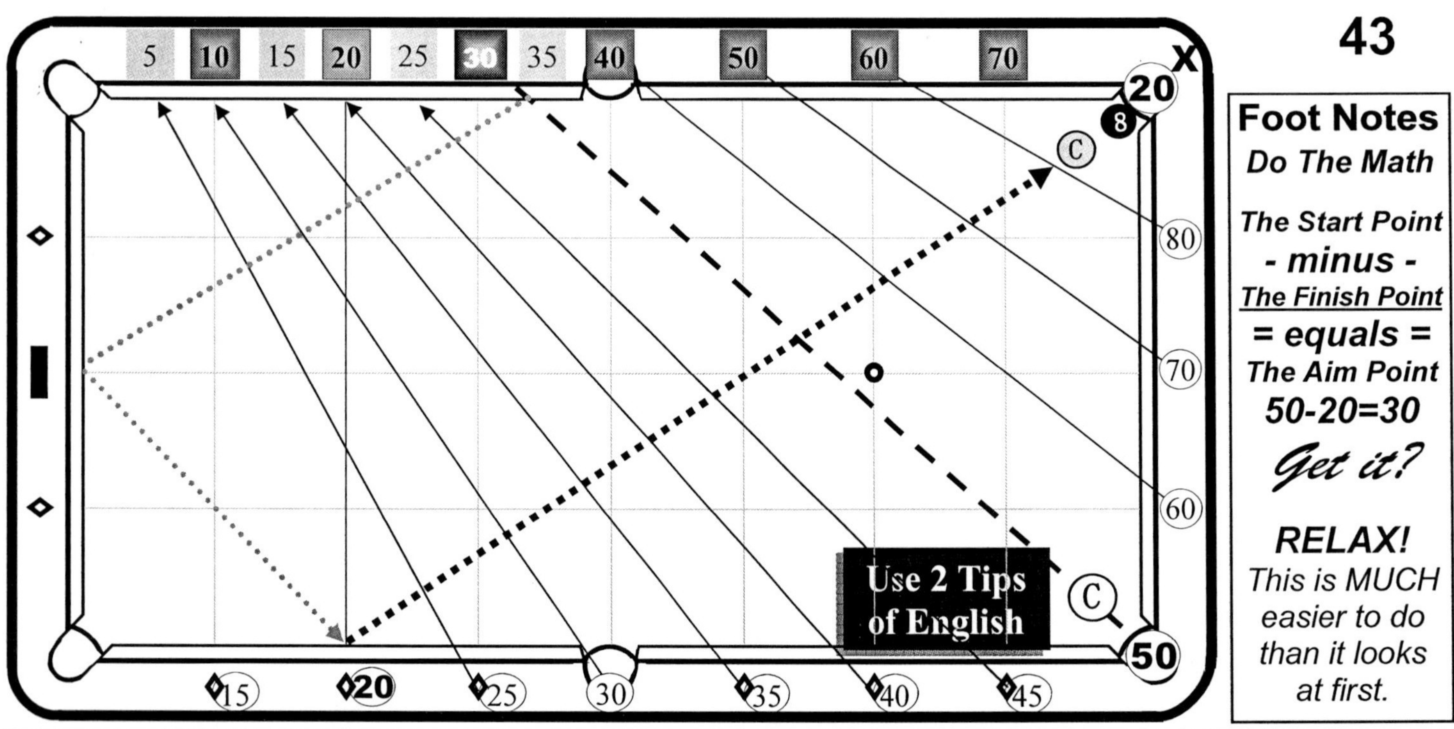

Foot Notes

Do The Math

The Start Point

- minus -

The Finish Point

= equals =

The Aim Point

50-20=30

Get it?

RELAX!

This is MUCH easier to do than it looks at first.

Advanced Option

Test shooting into the 20 Diamond with 1 Tip of English. This should also return to the **20** corner.

PROBLEM: 1. Where to shoot at the rail on a THREE rail KICK shot.

BASIC:

1. The first step is to know where the cue ball will finish. In this case, **X** is the finish point-pocketing the 8 Ball to win. The cue ball is coming off the last rail marked as (20) and heading for the corner pocket. ***Any ball coming off the 20 Diamond usually goes to the corner pocket*** (that'll explain a lot of your scratches).
2. The second step is to identify the ***Starting Track***. This starts at the cue ball. The starting *corner pocket* always has a point value of 50.
3. The third step is to take the value of the ***Starting Track*** (50), and subtract the destination track value (20). Do the math: **50 - 20 = 30**. ***Therefore, aim into the 30 Diamond on your Starting Track.***
4. Keep a level cue and use a 6 to 8 Speed Stroke.
5. Use 2 Tips of English with a smooth follow-through. Adjust the English if the rails are running Short or Long (I find many commercial tables run short).

Note: Shots from the 50 to 80 Diamond aim directly at the Diamond on the first rail.

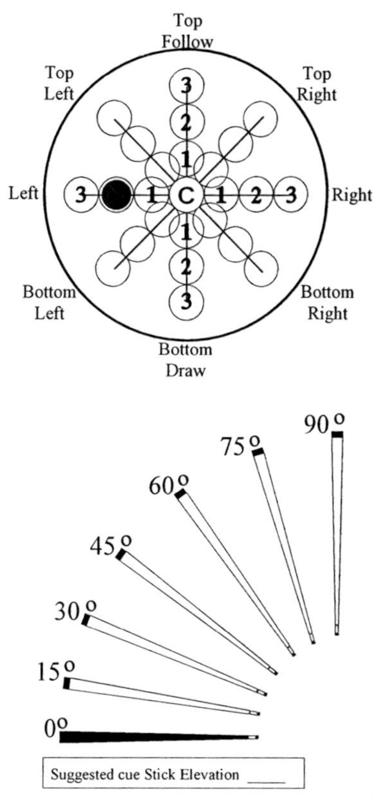

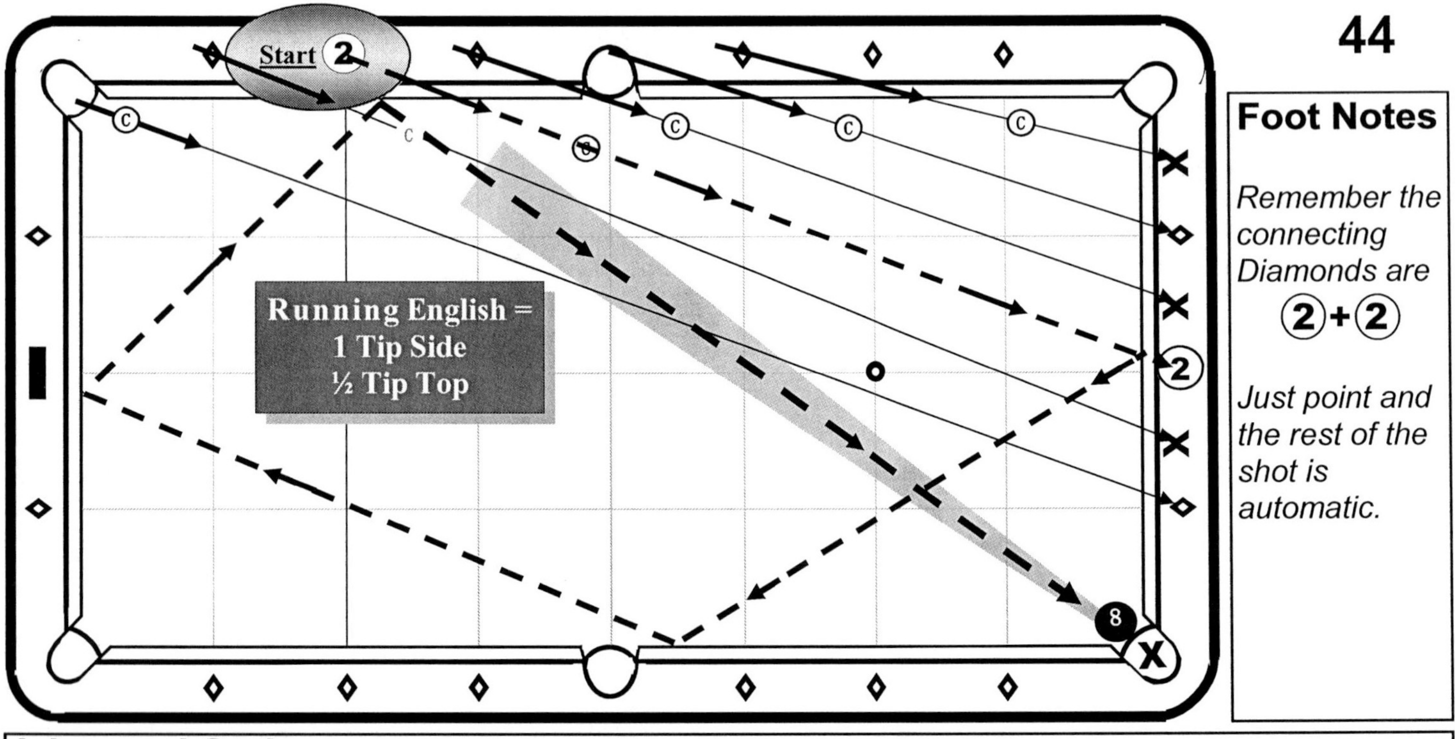

Foot Notes

Remember the connecting Diamonds are ②+②

Just point and the rest of the shot is automatic.

Advanced Option

1. Start from any of the Cue Ball Starting Tracks and aim at the First Rail Contact Points. Parallel Shift in between Diamonds.
2. Add more English to come short on the final pocket track.

PROBLEM: 1. Where to shoot at the rail on a FOUR Rail KICK Shot.

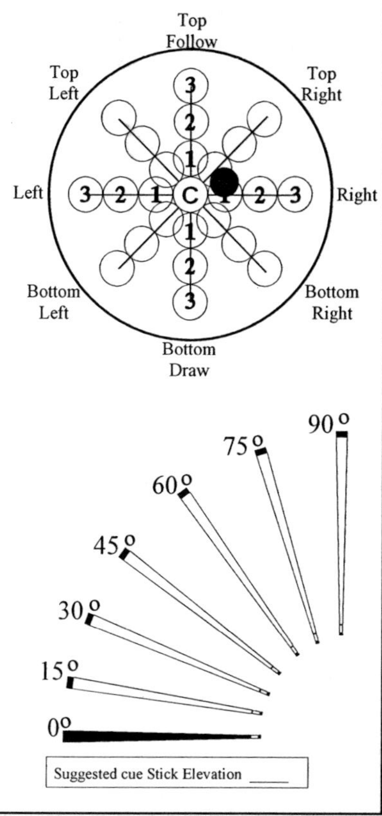

BASIC:

1. The first step is to know where the cue ball will finish. In this case, **X** is the finish point, pocketing the 8 Ball to win. The cue ball is coming off the last rail marked (2) and heading for the corner pocket.

2. The second step is to know where you're starting from. This is usually Cue Ball Starting Track. It's marked with (2).

3. Keep a level cue and use a 7 to 8 Speed Stroke.

4. Use Running English with a smooth follow-through. Adjust the English if the rails are running Short or Long.

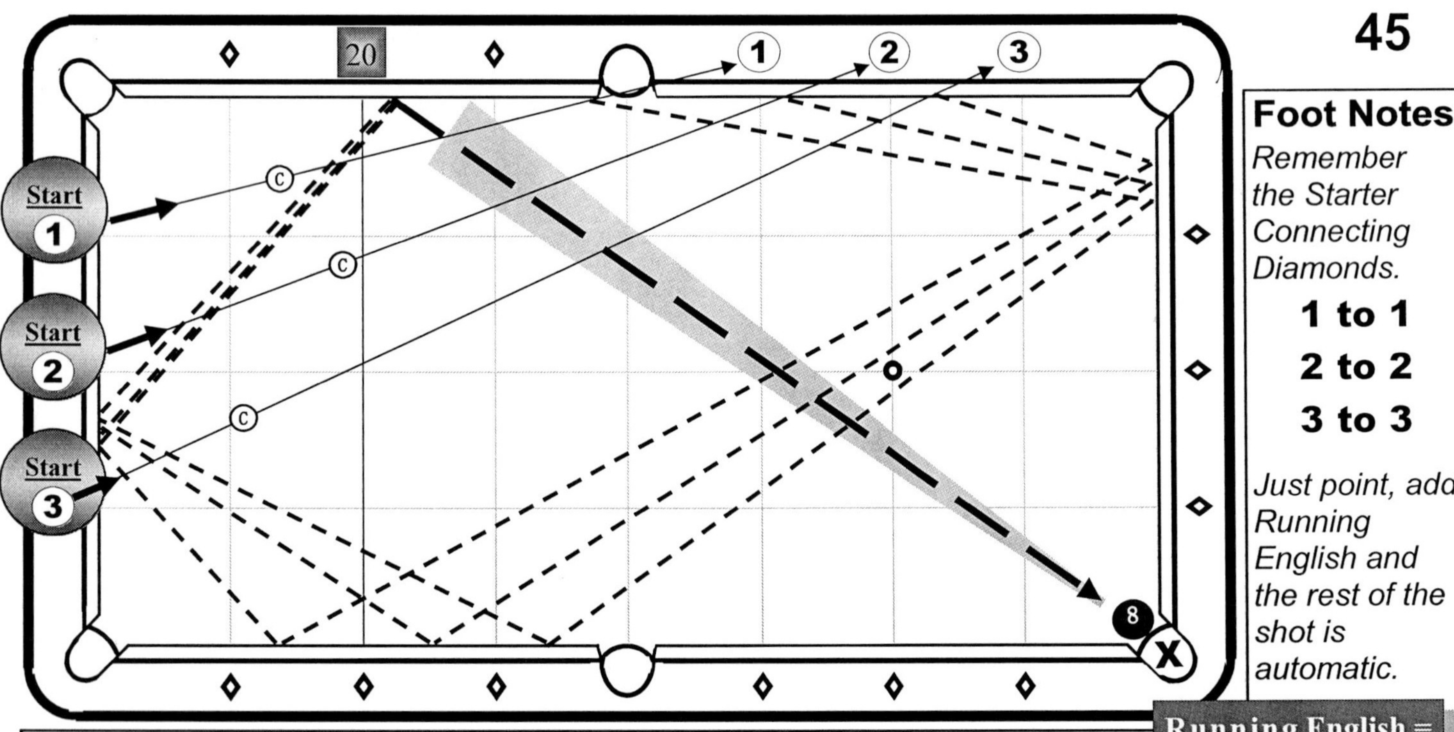

Foot Notes

Remember the Starter Connecting Diamonds.

1 to 1

2 to 2

3 to 3

Just point, add Running English and the rest of the shot is automatic.

Running English =
1 Tip Side
½ Tip Top

Advanced Option

1. Start from any of the Cue Ball *Starting Tracks* and aim at the First Rail Contact Points. Parallel Shift in between Diamonds.
2. Add more English to come short on the final pocket track.

PROBLEM: 1. Where to shoot at the rail on a FIVE Rail KICK Shot.

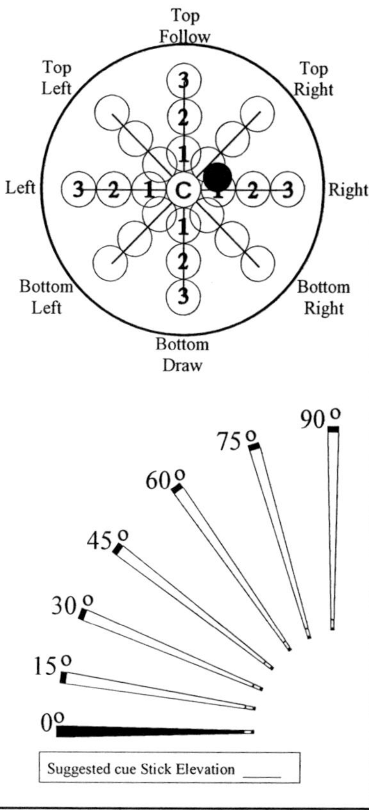

BASIC:

1. The first step is to know where the cue ball will finish. In this case, **X** is the finish point, pocketing the 8 Ball to win. The cue ball is coming off the last rail marked (20) and heading for the corner pocket.
2. The second step is to know where you're starting from. This is usually Cue Ball Starting Track. It's marked with (1) (2) and (3).
3. Keep a level cue and use a 7 to 8 Speed Stroke.
4. Use Running English with a smooth follow-through. Adjust the English if the rails are running Short or Long.

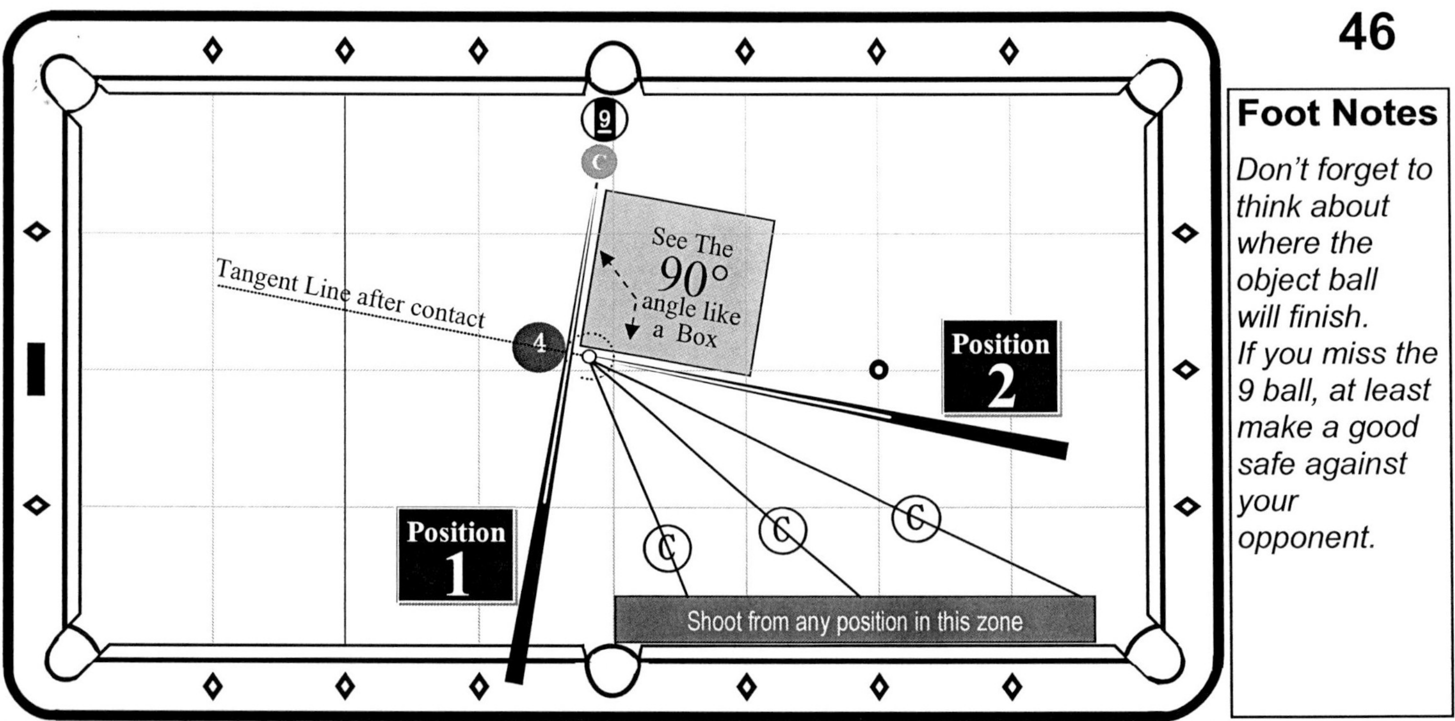

Foot Notes

Don't forget to think about where the object ball will finish.
If you miss the 9 ball, at least make a good safe against your opponent.

Advanced Option

Any Speed Stroke *(hitting the 4 ball above)* with ZERO SPIN, will Carom 90° from the contact Aim Spot.

PROBLEM: 1. How to carom to make the 9 ball hanging in the pocket.

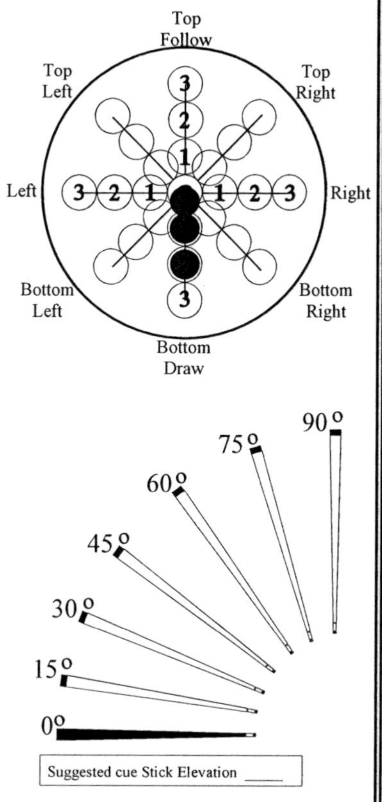

BASIC:

Step 1. From **Position 1** place the Tip of your cue at the base of the ball you want to contact or pocket (the 9 ball above).

Step 2. Bring the side of your cue next to the object ball you will carom off of, ***being very careful not to touch that ball with your cue stick.*** Make a mental note where the side of the cue shaft touches the object ball. That is the AIM SPOT you must shot at.

Step 3. Shoot the cue ball at the determined AIM SPOT being sure it has ZERO SPIN at the time it makes contact. Stroke Speeds may vary just as long as contact is made with ZERO SPIN.

NOTE: Working in **Position 2,** stand facing directly at the AIM SPOT placing the Tip of your cue at the base of the ball and see the 90° angle to pin-point the AIM SPOT on the object ball. Try to imagine seeing a box on the table. This helps to accurately see the 90° angle lines to the AIM SPOT.

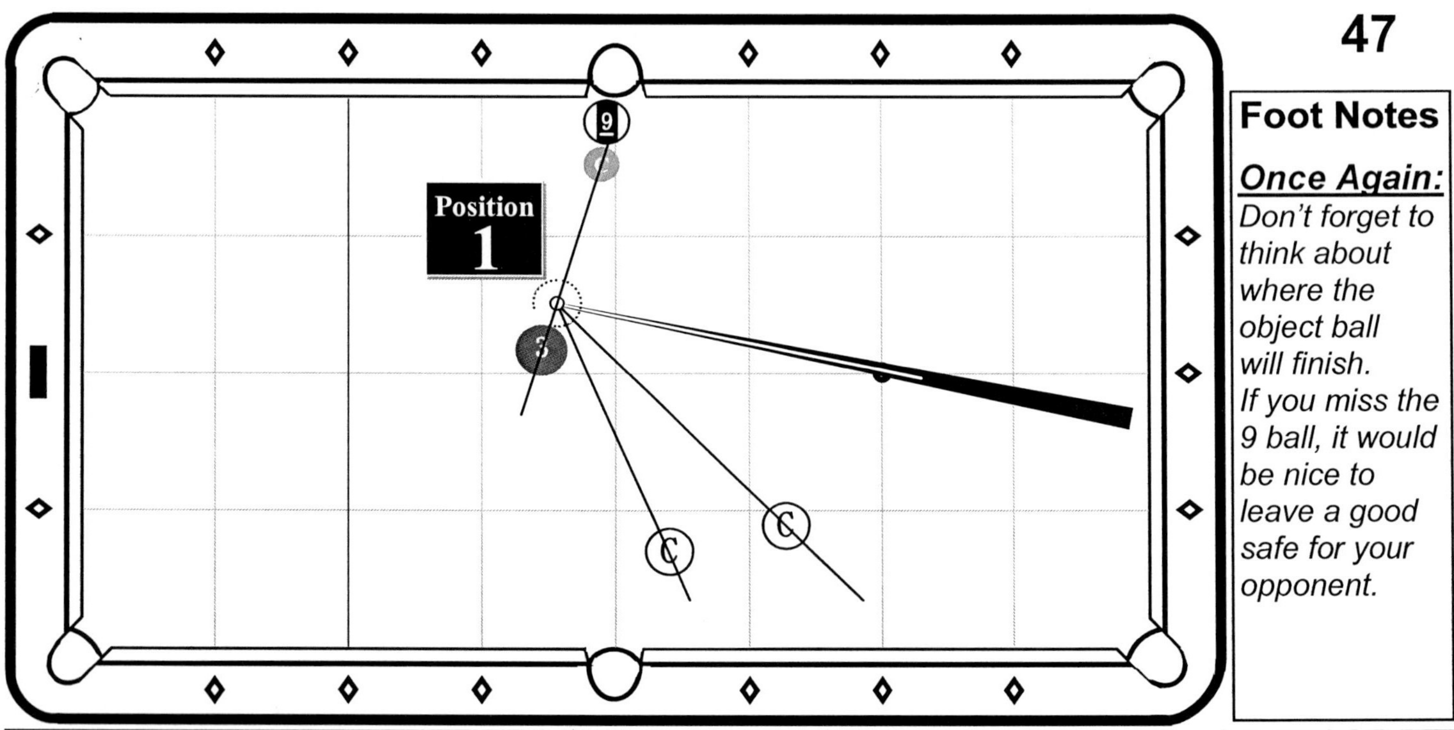

Foot Notes

Once Again:

Don't forget to think about where the object ball will finish.
If you miss the 9 ball, it would be nice to leave a good safe for your opponent.

Advanced Option

Adjust from Natural Roll to Draw based on the angle coming off the object ball.

PROBLEM: 1. How to carom off the first object ball and pocket the 9 ball hanging in the side (or corner) pocket.

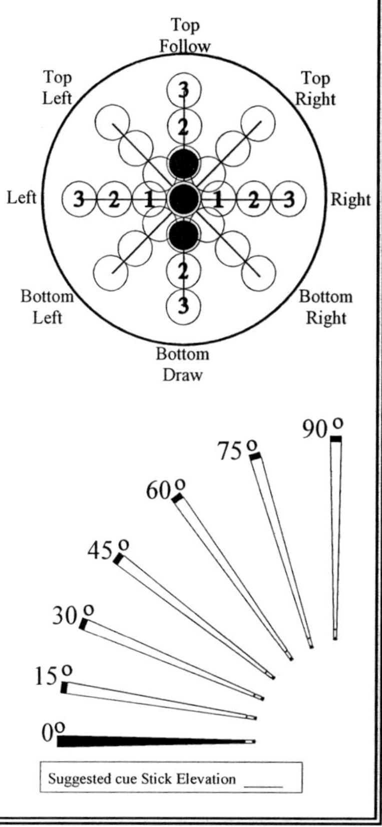

BASIC:

Step 1. From **Position 1** place the Tip of your cue at the base of the **Ghost Ball** position that is in line with the 9 ball (see above).

Step 2. Make a mental note of that spot. That is the AIM SPOT you'll be shooting at.

Step 3. Shoot the cue ball at the Ghost Ball AIM SPOT, being sure it has NATURAL ROLL at the time it makes contact with the object ball. Stroke Speeds may vary just as long as contact is made with NATURAL ROLL at the time of contact.

NOTE: You can use both line-up aiming systems in shots 46 and 47 to cross-check each other if it is critical that you don't miss. All that changes is the cue ball English.

47 CAROM FOLLOW SHOT 2

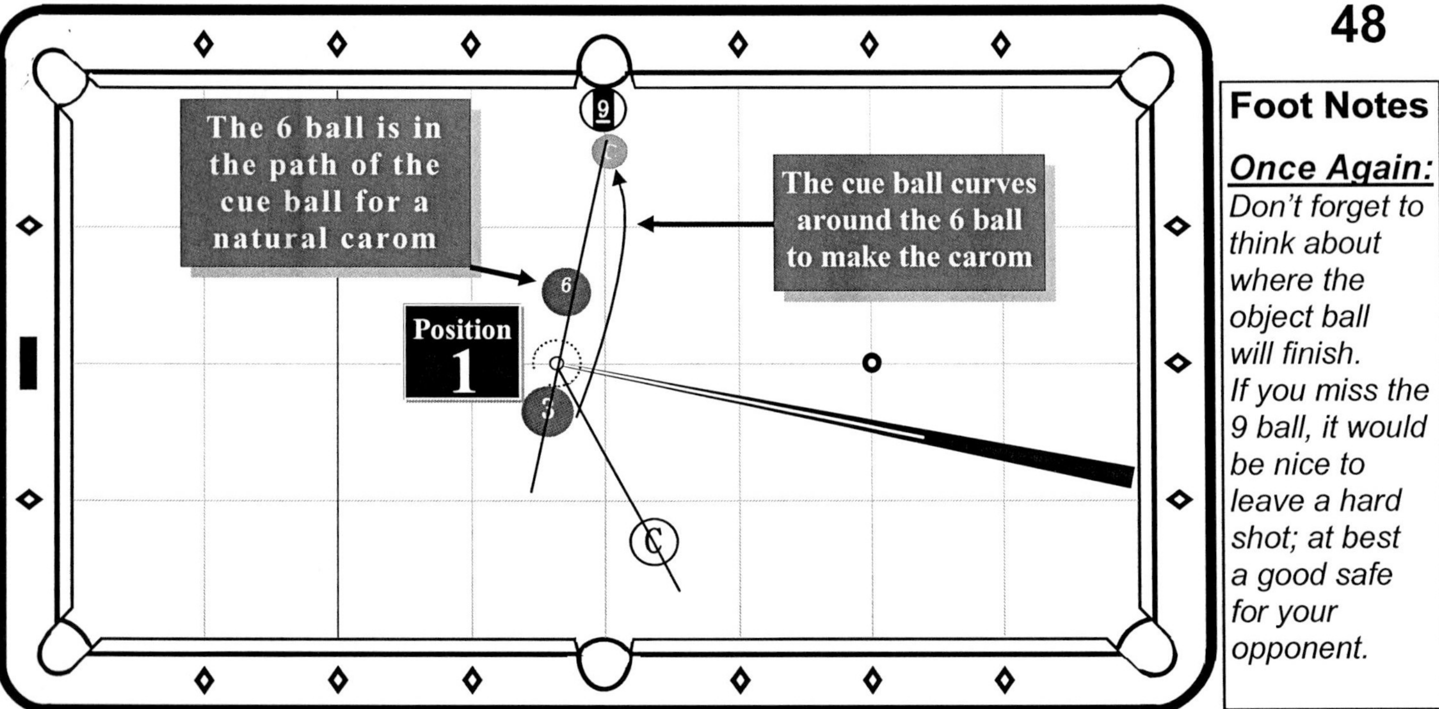

Foot Notes

Once Again:
Don't forget to think about where the object ball will finish. If you miss the 9 ball, it would be nice to leave a hard shot; at best a good safe for your opponent.

Advanced Option

Use a 5 to 7 Speed Stroke (*hitting the 3 ball above*) with Top SPIN, will curve the Carom to the contact Aim Spot.

PROBLEM: 1. The 9 ball hanging in the side pocket is being blocked by another object ball, preventing a regular Carom shot.

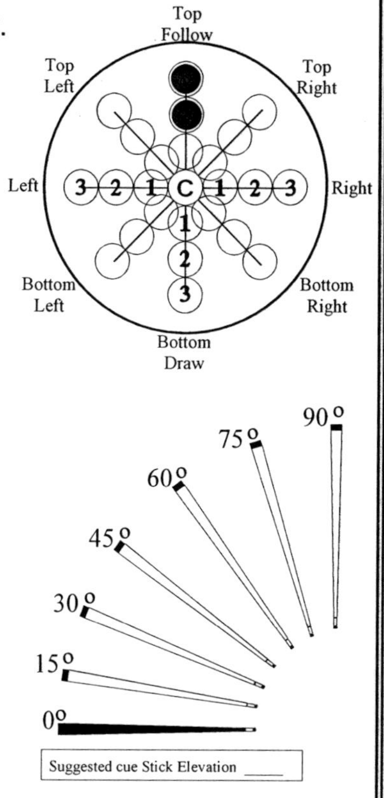

BASIC:

Step 1. From **Position 1** place the Tip of your cue at the base of the **Ghost Ball** position that is in line with the 9 ball (see above).

Step 2. Make a mental note of that spot. That is the AIM SPOT you'll be shooting at.

Step 3. Shoot the cue ball at the Ghost Ball AIM SPOT being sure it has TOP SPIN at the time it makes contact with the object ball. Stroke Speeds may vary just as long as contact is made with TOP SPIN.

NOTE: TOP SPIN / Follow English can vary between 2 to 3 Tips depending on the angle shooting into the object ball and the distance between the first object ball hit and the second ball hit.

 CAROM CURVE FOLLOW SHOT

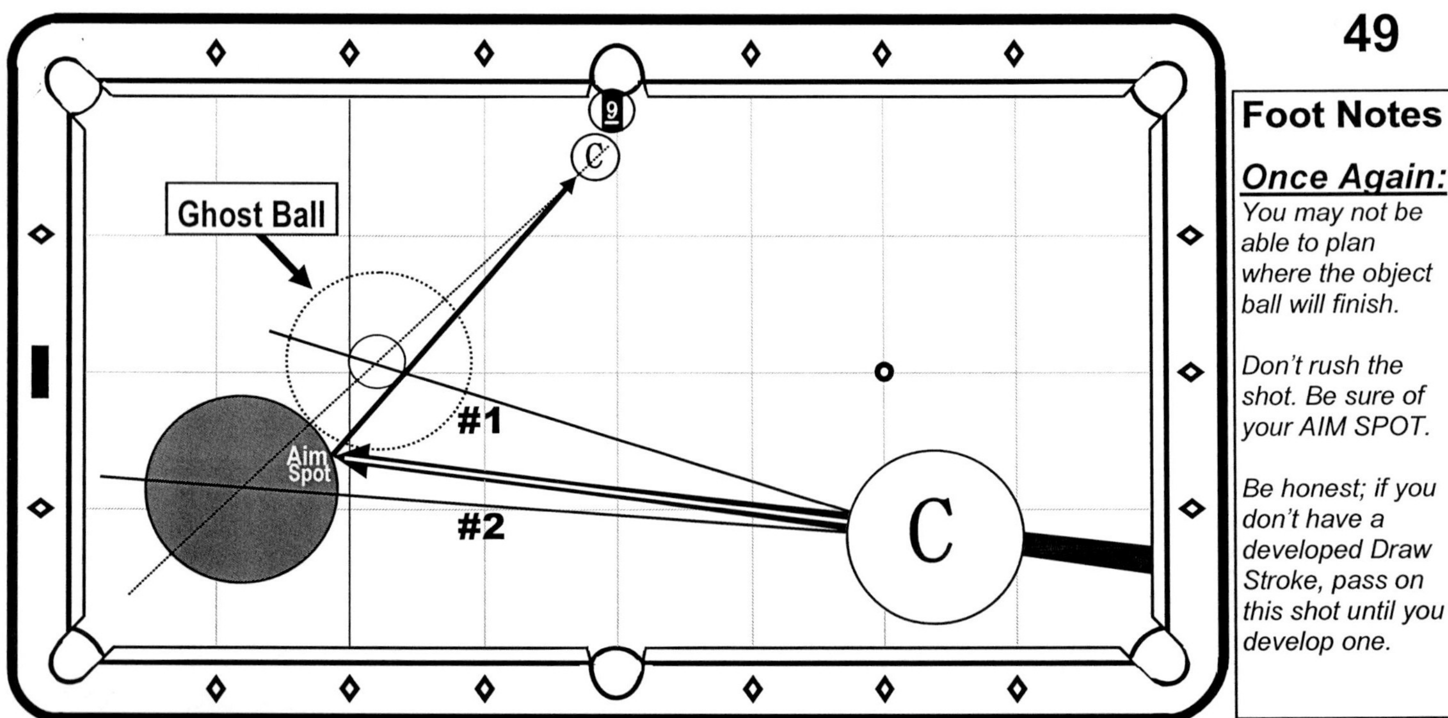

Foot Notes

Once Again:

You may not be able to plan where the object ball will finish.

Don't rush the shot. Be sure of your AIM SPOT.

Be honest; if you don't have a developed Draw Stroke, pass on this shot until you develop one.

Advanced Option

Adjust your Draw stroke speed based on the distance to, and coming off, the first object ball.

PROBLEM: 1. How to DRAW off an object ball into another ball (*making the 9 ball hanging in the side pocket*).

BASIC:

Step 1. Line **#1** is the base of the Ghost Ball position that is in line with the 9 ball (see above). That is the 1st Set-Up Spot.

Step 2. Line **#2** is a line directly through the object ball (see above). That is the 2nd Set-Up Spot you'll need to see.

Step 3. Line **#3** is the AIM SPOT. It is directly between the first two points on the object ball. Shoot at that spot with whatever amount of DRAW Stroke you desire to use.

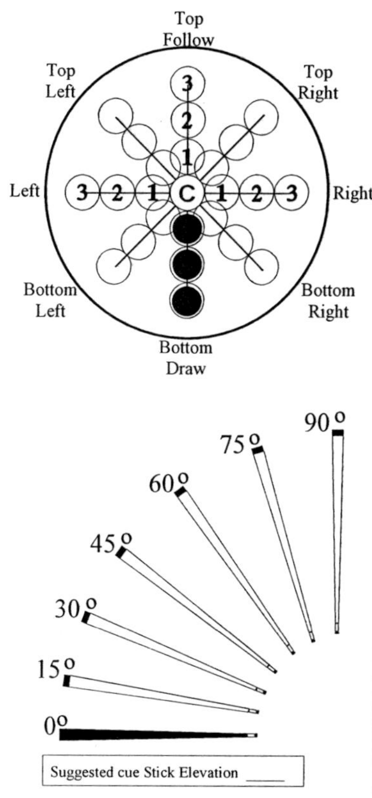

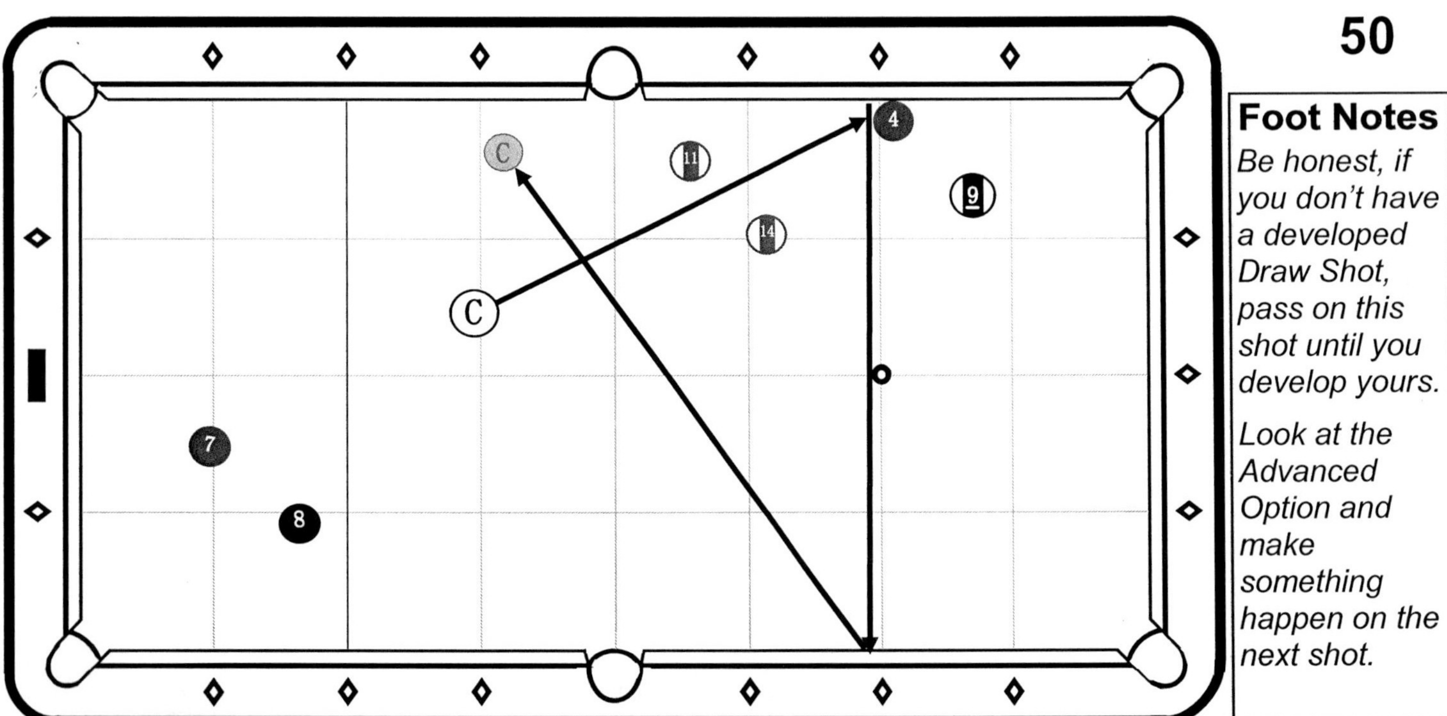

50

Foot Notes

Be honest, if you don't have a developed Draw Shot, pass on this shot until you develop yours.

Look at the Advanced Option and make something happen on the next shot.

Advanced Option

Sometimes you just come out enough to see the next ball. Bear down and come with a good shot.

PROBLEM: 1. You can't draw directly out of the rail to get back up table.

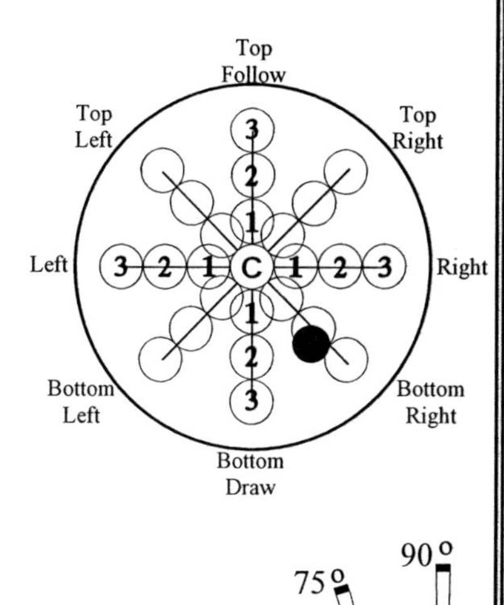

BASIC:

Step 1. Aim at the object (4 ball) to pocket it in the corner pocket.

Step 2. Use 2 Tips Bottom (inside) Right.

Step 3. Level cue and full follow-through with a 7 to 8 Speed Stroke.

This shot is beautiful when executed correctly.

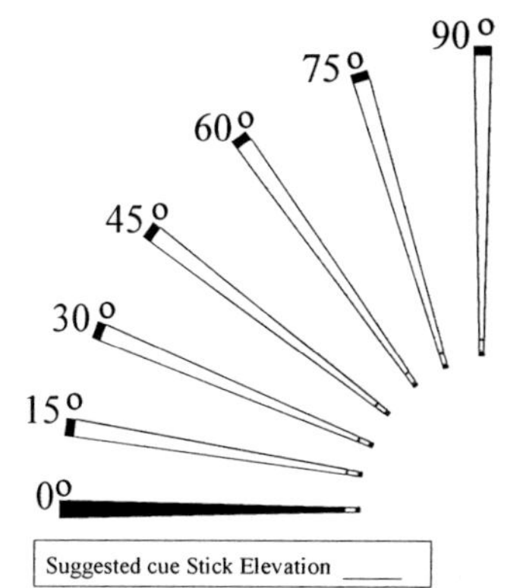

50 ACROSS AND BACK UP DRAW SHOT

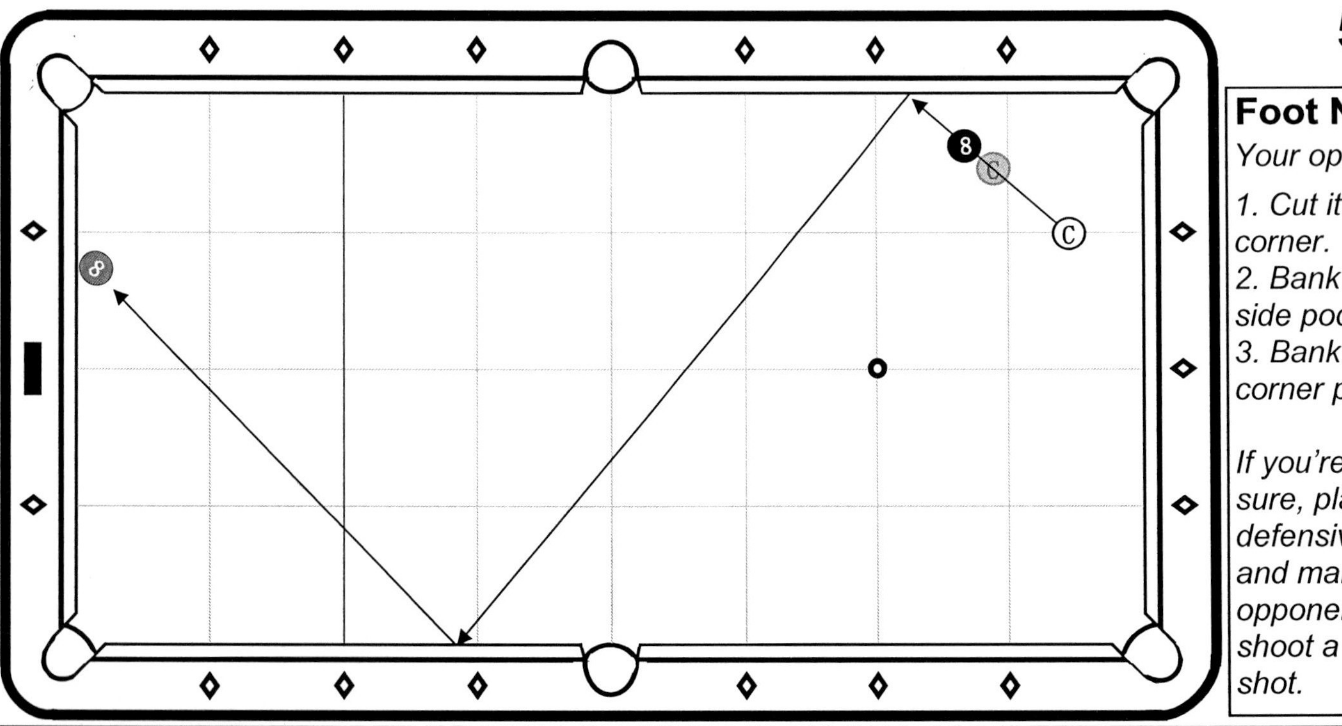

Foot Notes

Your option is:

1. Cut it up the corner.
2. Bank in the side pocket.
3. Bank in the corner pocket.

If you're not sure, play defensively and make your opponent shoot a hard shot.

Advanced Option

Draw the cue ball back to the bottom rail so if the 8 ball is open, the next shot is off the rail.

PROBLEM: 1. Cut shot is too hard to make.
2. Bank shots are blocked or too hard to make.

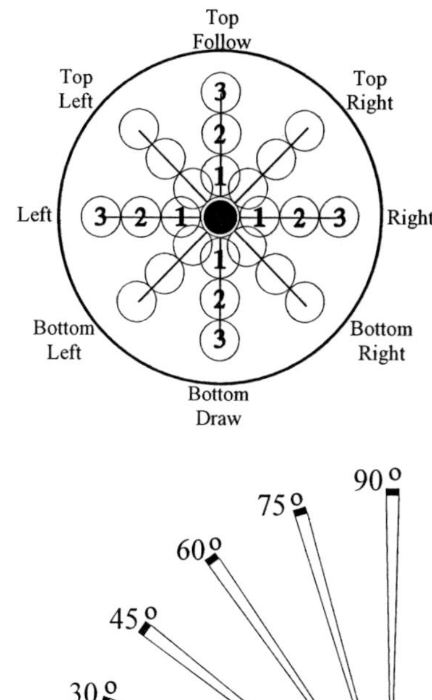

BASIC:

Step 1. Shoot the object ball directly into the rail.

Step 2. Use Center English or 1 Tip Below Center.

Step 3. Level cue and full follow-through with a 6 Speed Stroke.

This safety shot transfers the problem back to your opponent.

51 PASSING THE HARD SHOT BACK 1

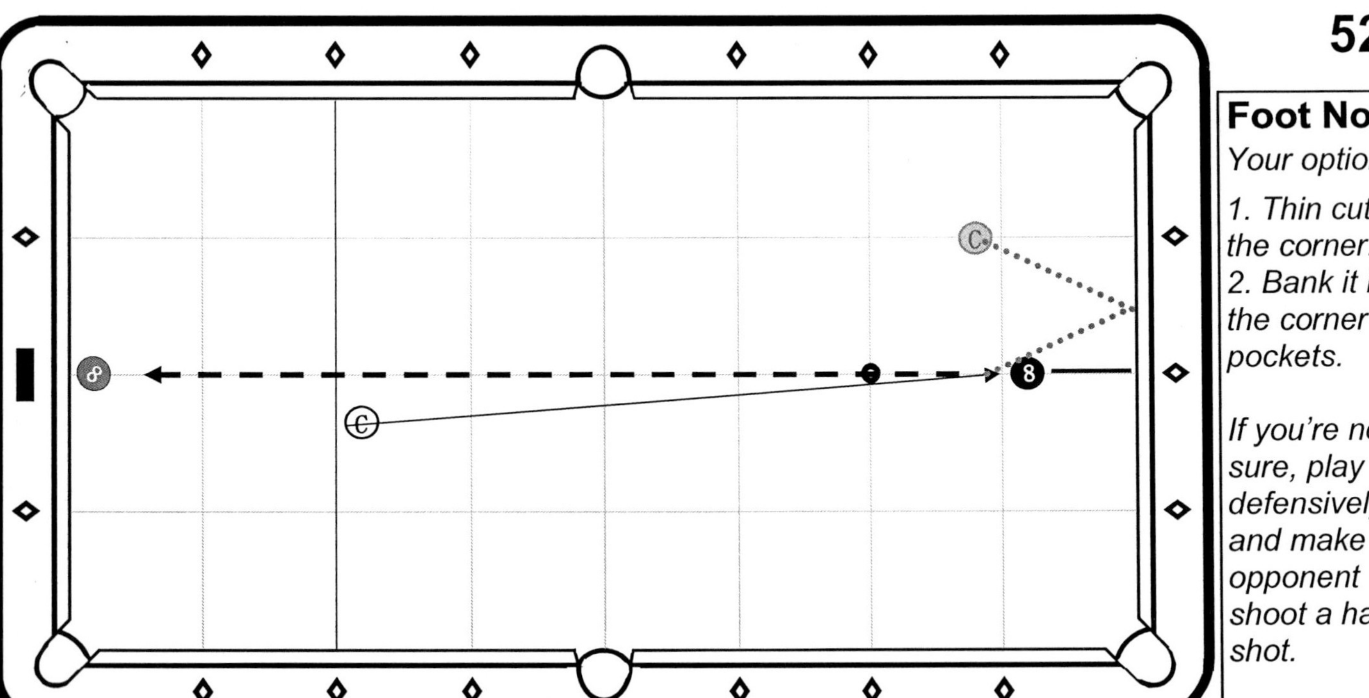

Foot Notes

Your option is:

1. Thin cut it in the corner.
2. Bank it in the corner pockets.

If you're not sure, play defensively and make your opponent shoot a hard shot.

Advanced Option

Slow roll the 8 ball into the bottom rail then up table to the opposite rail. The cue ball will roll out.

PROBLEM: 1. Cut shot is too hard to make.
2. Bank shots are blocked or too hard to make.

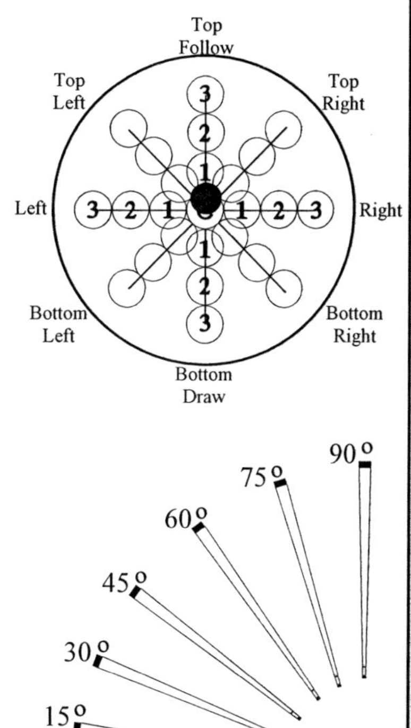

BASIC:

Step 1. Shoot the object ball directly into the rail, then back up to the opposite rail.

Step 2. Use ½ Tip above Center English for a natural roll.

Step 3. Use a level cue and full follow-through

Step 4. Use about a 4 Speed Stroke.

This safety shot transfers the problem back to your opponent.

This is one of the single most effective ways to escape the pressure of shooting a hard shot.

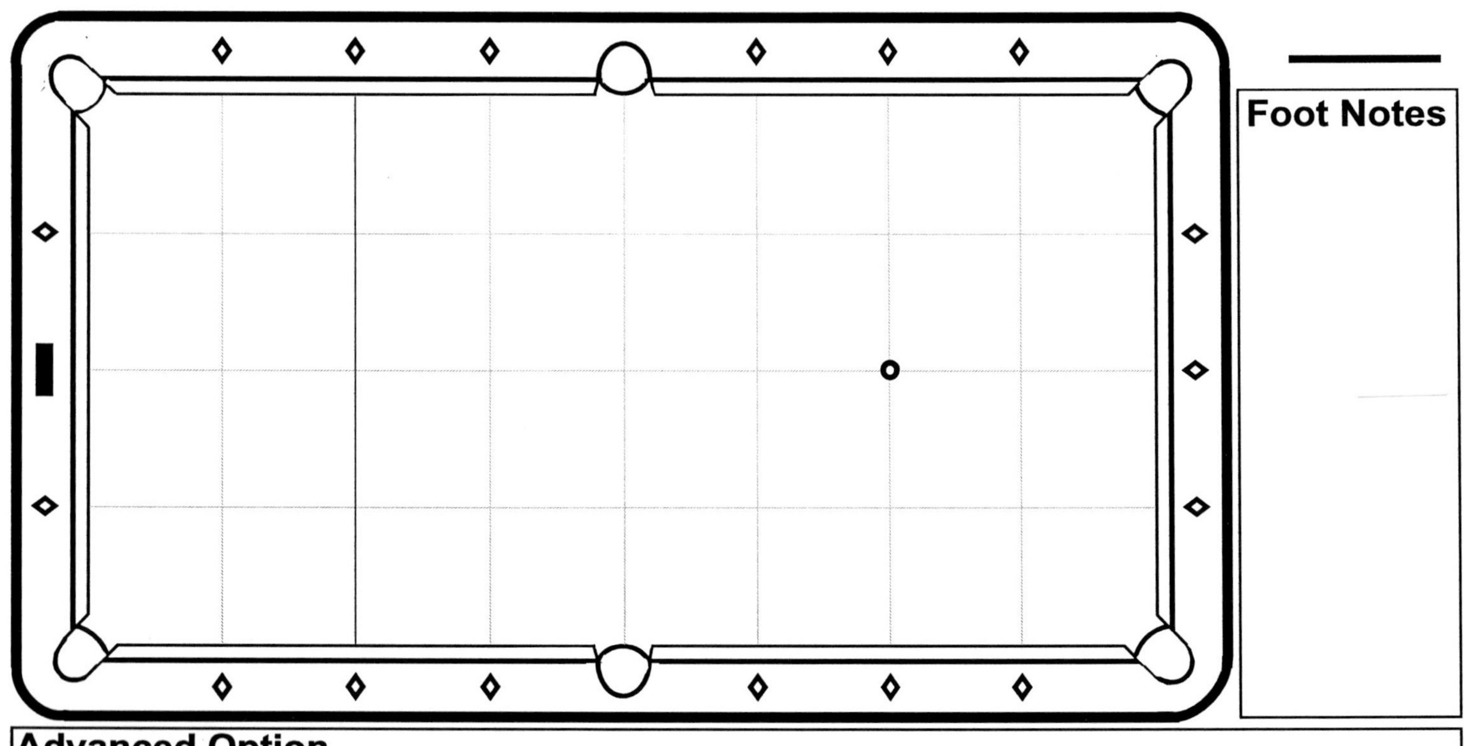

Foot Notes

Advanced Option

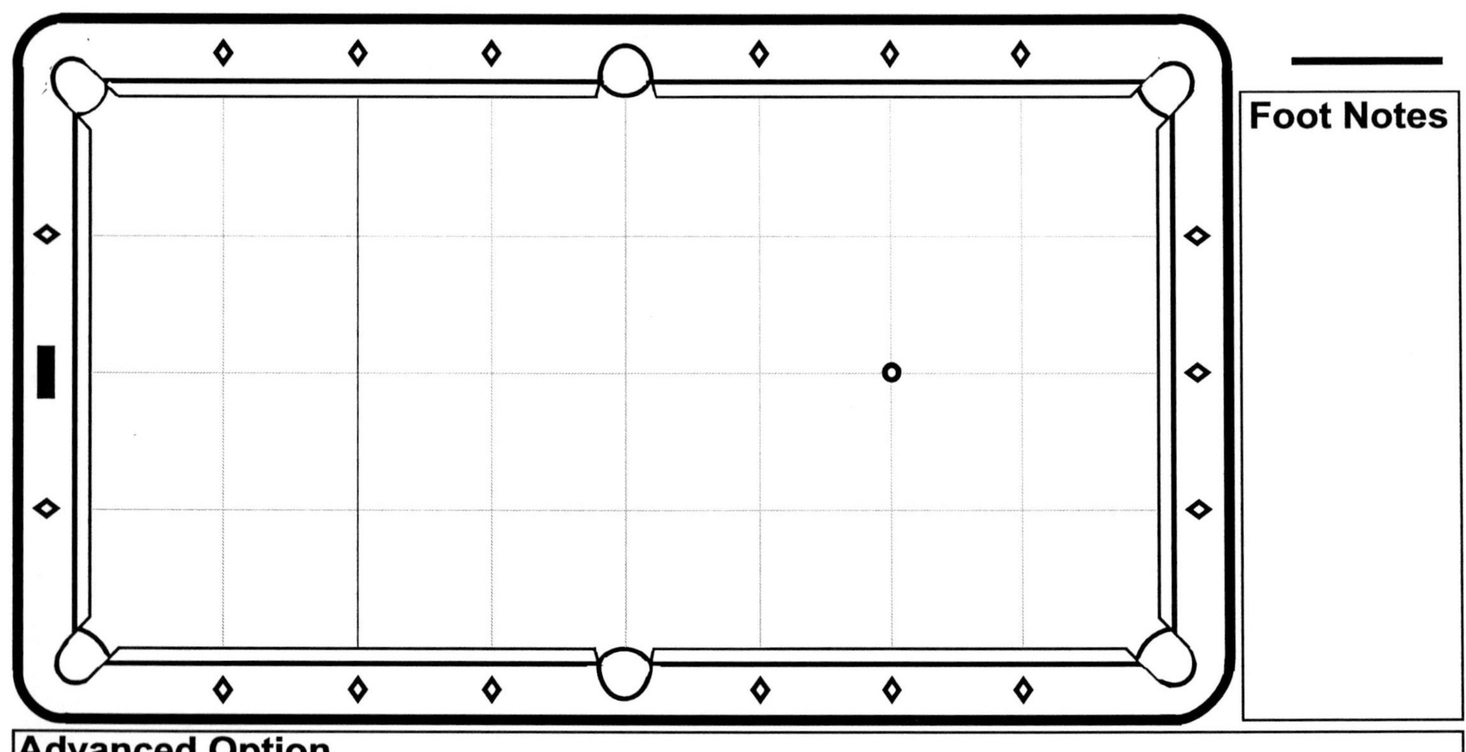

Foot Notes

Advanced Option

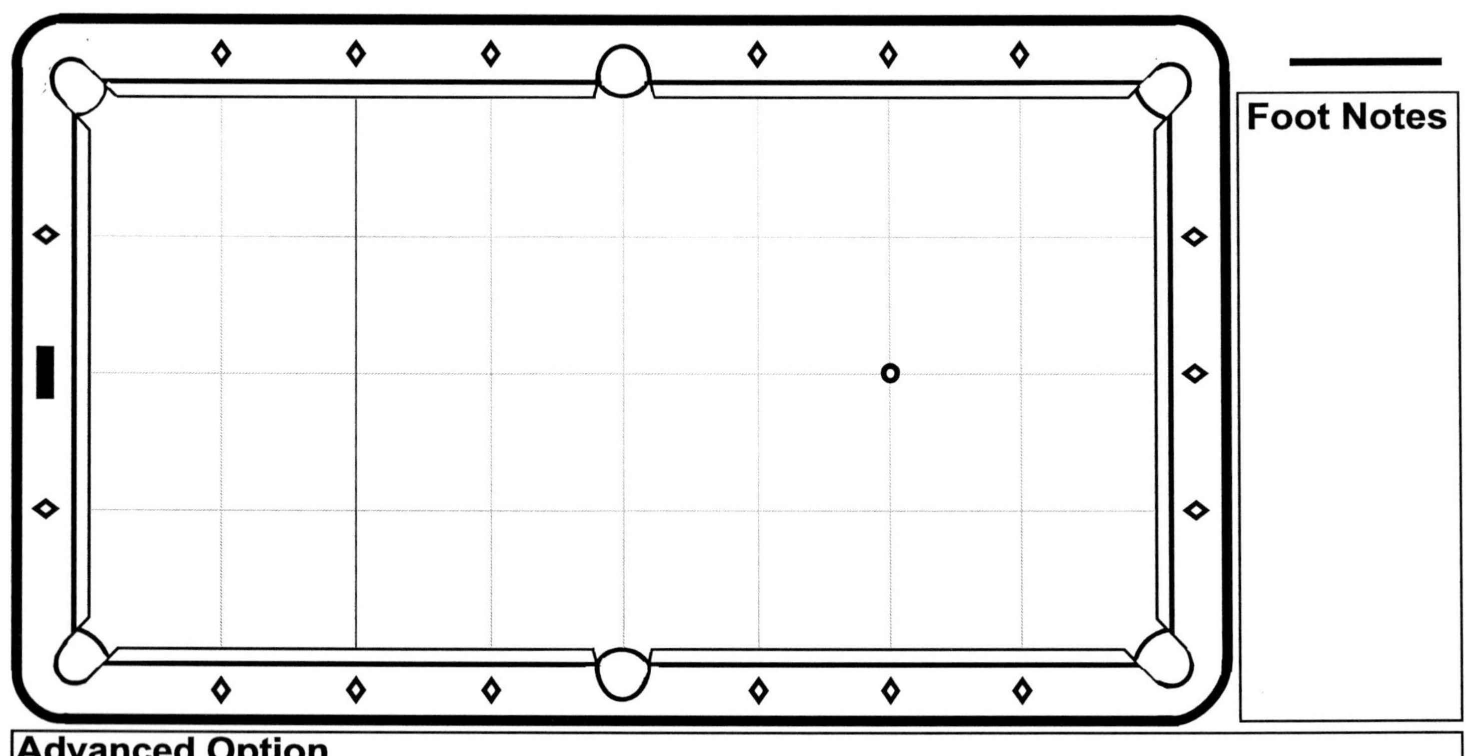

Foot Notes

Advanced Option

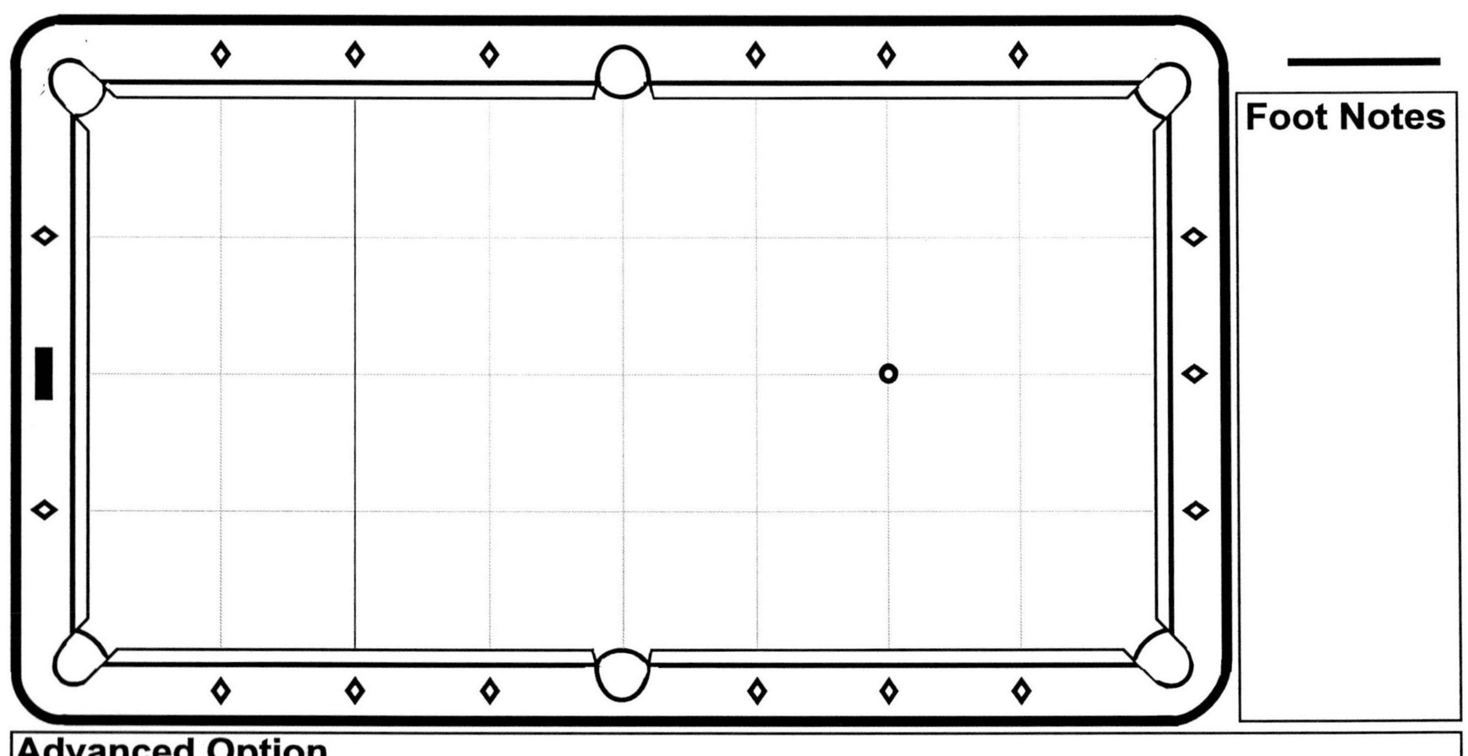

Foot Notes

Advanced Option

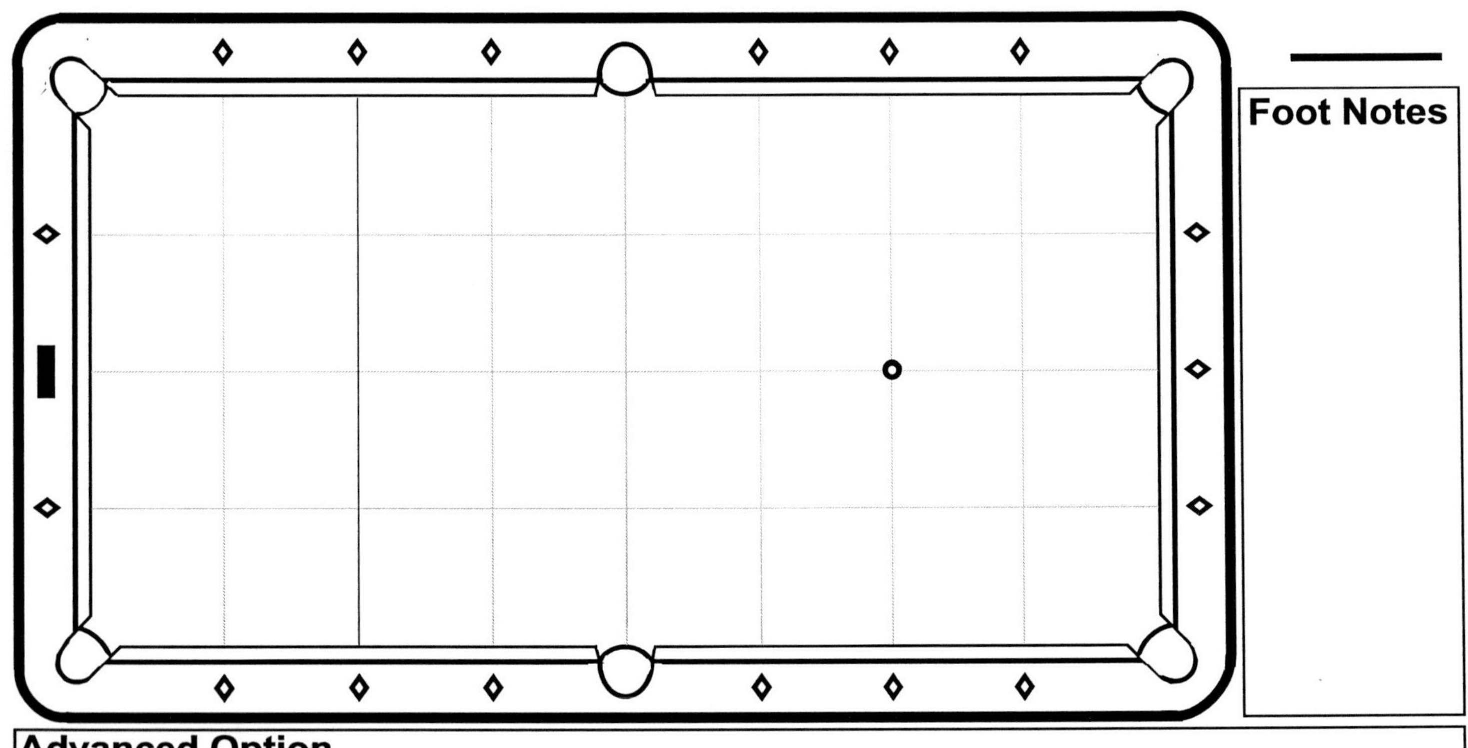

Foot Notes

Advanced Option

Published in the United States by ROCK SOLID. Proceeds from this work are used to fund ministry expenses which provide counseling, teaching and other useful materials. Ministry includes, but is not limited to, assisting individuals with practical life needs when there is sufficiency to provide.

Library of Congress Cataloging-in-Publication Data,

THE DRILL INSTRUCTOR, Esposito, Dominic M. 1956-

2nd Printing

TIME OUT Pool League Shots

52 Drills with Over 150 Shots

1. Pool (Game)

For private instruction, group clinics, exhibitions or personal contact,

E-mail: Dominic@ProSkillDrills.com

Web Page: www.ProSkillDrills.com

Telephone in the USA: 1-407-927-1484 or

Write to:

Pro Skill Drills, 6541 Pomeroy Circle, Orlando, FL, 32810

Manufactured in the United States of America

15 14 13 12 11 10 9 8 7 6 5 4 3 2 1 C

To God Be The Glory and Honor

To Our Families Be The Affection

To Our Friends Be The Memories

To Our Teachers Be The Gratitude

To The Game of Pool - Be The Ball

To All You Who Use Pro Skill Drills

- Thank You

In Loving Memory of Cleveland, Ohio

Pocket Billiard Champion

Thomas P. Parker

1921 - 1989

A True Gentleman, Friend, and My Pool Mentor

Special Thanks To My Bride Linda, I Love You.

This wouldn't be if not for you.

Book Only

Pro Skill Drills Vol. 3, *The Practice Session Record Keeper*.

Keep a journal of your practice sessions, goals and shot making improvement. Personal statistics of your practice and playing time will keep you on the winning track, while at the same time reveal potential problem areas before they adversely affect your game. Includes over 150 pages of blank table grids and practice statistic journal pages.

Pro Skill Drills Vol. 4, *The 27 Practicing Secrets of the Pros*

teaches you to create a pre-practice, practice, and post-practice routine that will maximize your time and form a game plan, while driving you to build up every area of your game. This material will fully prepare you for the physical, mental and emotional demands of *Pro* competition.

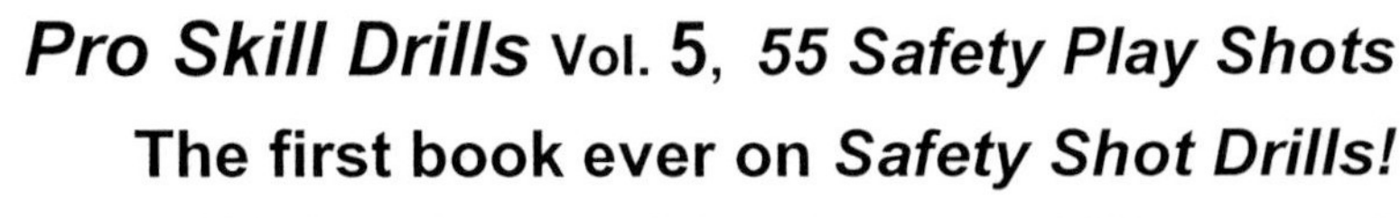

Pro Skill Drills Vol. 5, *55 Safety Play Shots*

The first book ever on *Safety Shot Drills!*

Do you fall short in your defensive game? Do you sell out shots that give your opponent the opportunity to run out on you? Practicing these safety drills will teach you all the defensive skills you need to keep control of the table, think your way out of tough situations, and get you ball-in-hand more often.

These is the #1 Drill Books & DVDs In all the world!

Pro Skill Drills Vol. 6, *54 ONE POCKET Practice Session Drills!*

Arm yourself with all the advanced shots you need to play One Pocket. Learn shots that come up over and over, game after game. Fully illustrated, spiral-bound design. DVD bonus footage on playing through the rack.

BOOT CAMP *Pro Skill Drills Vol.* 7

52 TACTICAL DRILLS for Aiming, Kicking, Banking, Jumping, Warm-Ups, Plus the revolutionary

PREDATOR-EYES AIMING SYSTEM

If you've hit a plateau, you're in a slump or you're rusty from not playing for several years, this is exactly what you'll need to develop a complete and well-rounded game. With the book and over 3 Hours on DVD, The Drill Instructor will *Challenge* and *Empower* you with practical, first hand coaching that will build you up and take your pool playing skills to their top level. ***It's Guaranteed to work if you do!***

***BOOT CAMP** makes playing and competing at pool more fun than ever before!*

Vol. 8, TIME OUT is: The Pool Shot BIBLE

Through 52 Drills You'll Learn Over 150 Shots.

Vol. 8 is "**HOW TO SHOOT"** all the hard shots in pool! Each shot is taught in basic language so lower ranked players can understand. Yet each shot provides options for the top level player. You'll discover how pros think when they call for an "Extension." Many of these shots are secrets road hustlers have used to win. You'll learn shots many "instructors" don't teach.

<u>I've taught these shots to pros and now I'll teach them to you!</u>

Jester2

DEFINITIONS

<u>Running English:</u> 1 Tip (left or right side) English then ½ Tip Top (above) Center. If the cue ball bounces to the right after hitting the first rail, apply the SPIN to the right side. If the cue ball bounces to the left after hitting the first rail, apply the SPIN to the left side of the cue ball.

<u>Soft English:</u> 1 Tip above center then ⅛ to ¼ Tip (left or right side) English. If the cue ball bounces to the right after hitting the first rail, apply the SPIN to the right side. If the cue ball bounces to the left after hitting the first rail, apply the SPIN to the left side of the cue ball.

<u>Speed Stroke:</u>
From the top rail, each half table length counts for one Speed Stroke.

The numbers ZigZag to show each Speed Zone. Always shoot in a straight line on all speed strokes.

<u>1 2 3 = SLOW Speeds</u>
<u>4 5 6 = MEDIUM Speeds</u>
<u>7 8 9 = HARD Speeds</u>
<u>10 = BREAK Speed</u>

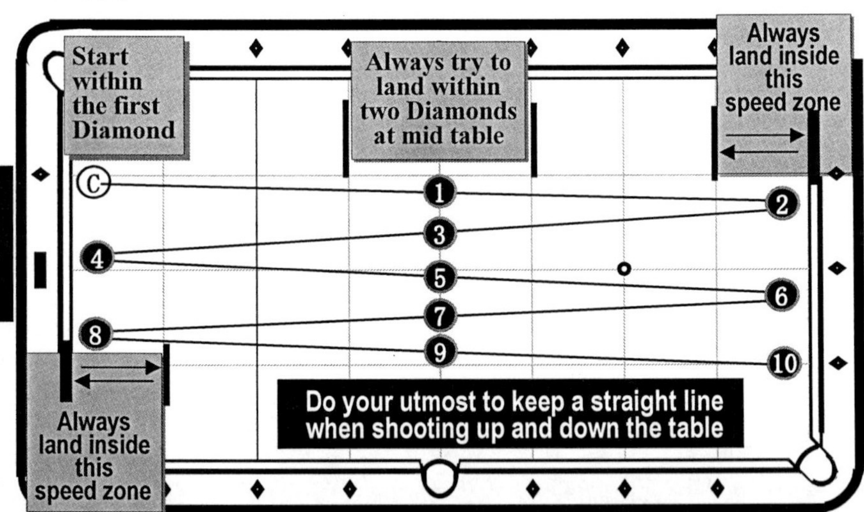

Diamond Starting Point = DSP: The position which the cue ball will be shot from.

Diamond Contact Point = DCP: The spot on the first rail the cue ball is being aimed to hit.

Diamond Target Point = DTP: The destination point of the cue ball.

Contact Point: The spot on the cue ball that makes contact with an object ball.

Aim Spot: The spot aimed at on an object ball that causes it to roll in an intended direction.

Double Kiss: The Tip of the playing cue or two balls that hit twice from a single stroke.

Frozen: When two or more balls, not moving, are touching or a ball is touching a rail.

Kick Shot: Shooting the cue ball into a rail first before hitting an intended object ball.

Kill Shot: Applying a draw SPIN that releases at the moment of contact with a ball or rail.

Parallel Shift: Holding the cue stick level, about a foot over the table, evenly sliding the entire cue stick to the left or right until reaching a desired cue or object ball track.

Perpendicular: The point where two balls or a ball to a rail are directly across from each other.

Jack Up: Elevating the butt of the cue while shooting.

English: The Tip of the playing cue hits the cue ball **anywhere** other than in the center. Up to 3 Tips of English can be applied to a cue ball with the Tip of a cue stick.

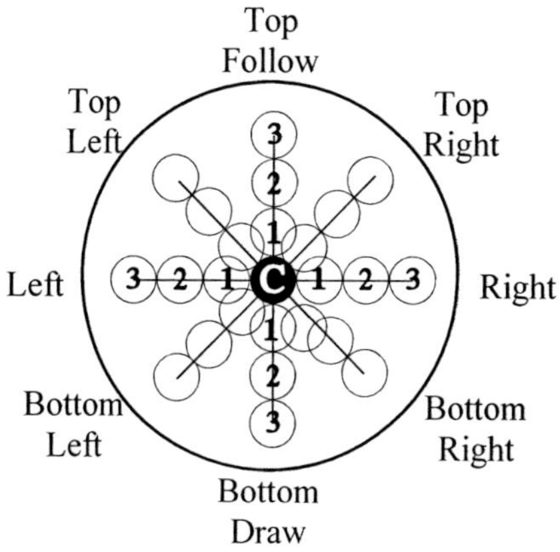

Top
Follow
Top
Left
Top
Right
3
2
1
Left
3 2 1 C 1 2 3
Right
1
2
3
Bottom
Left
Bottom
Right
Bottom
Draw